Guns or Growth?
Assessing the impact of arms sales on sustainable development

Jane Chanaa

Practical Action Publishing Ltd
25 Albert Street, Rugby, CV21 2SD, Warwickshire, UK
www.practicalactionpublishing.com

First edition published by Oxfam, 2004
This edition published by Practical Action Publishing Ltd, 2015

A catalogue record for this book is available from the British Library.
A catalogue record for this book has been requested from the Library of Congress.

ISBN-10: 0855985380
ISBN-13: 978-0855985387
Ebook ISBN:9780855987626
Book DOI: http://dx.doi.org/10.3362/9780855987626

Since 1974, Practical Action Publishing has published and disseminated books and information in support of international development work throughout the world. Practical Action Publishing is a trading name of Practical Action Publishing Ltd (Company Reg. No. 1159018), the wholly owned publishing company of Practical Action. Practical Action Publishing trades only in support of its parent charity objectives and any profits are covenanted back to Practical Action (Charity Reg. No. 247257, Group VAT Registration No. 880 9924 76).

The views and opinions in this publication are those of the author and do not represent those of Practical Action Publishing Ltd or its parent charity Practical Action. Reasonable efforts have been made to publish reliable data and information, but the authors and publisher cannot assume responsibility for the validity of all materials or for the consequences of their use.

Guns or Growth?

Assessing the impact of arms sales on sustainable development

Appendices 73

Summary

Excessive or inappropriate arms purchases are a drain on social and economic resources which developing countries cannot afford. Article 51 of the United Nations Charter recognises that every state has a right to individual and collective self-defence. However, the UN Charter also requires all member states to 'promote universal respect for, and observance of, human rights and freedoms' in order to achieve 'economic and social progress and development' (Articles 1, 55 and 56) and 'to promote the establishment and maintenance of international peace and security with the least diversion for armaments of the world's human and economic resources' (Article 26). A majority of states have, in addition, ratified the International Covenant on Economic, Social and Cultural Rights to contribute to the progressive realisation of these rights through international assistance and co-operation.

The Millennium Development Goals (MDGs) agreed in September 2000 by all 189 UN member states will not be achieved if resources are diverted from this vital task by inappropriate arms transfers. According to James Wolfensohn, president of the World Bank, there is a 'fundamental imbalance' with the world spending US$900bn on defence; around US$325bn on agricultural subsidies and only US$50bn to US$60bn on aid.

The countries of Africa, Latin America, Asia, and the Middle East hold 51 per cent of the world's heavy weapons. Both arms importers and exporters must ensure that arms transfers do not undermine sustainable development – a combination of economic growth and social progress that meets the needs of the present without compromising the ability of future generations to meet their own needs. For arms exporters, various export-control regimes already include this requirement, as does the proposed Arms Trade Treaty. However, it is shocking how **few governments make a serious attempt to consider the impact on development of their arms exports.** Paying lip service to such a commitment means that scarce resources are being diverted from the fight against poverty, and millions are suffering as a result. To protect the social and economic rights of people in developing countries, it is imperative that exporting governments apply an effective and systematic methodology to assess whether proposed arms transfers will affect sustainable development.

The assessment methodology must recognise that the potential consequences of an arms transfer are not always clear-cut, and weigh these consequences alongside the legitimate security needs of the country and respect for international human rights standards in the governance of its people. In many cases, countries that import arms may have legitimate security needs. However, the costs of meeting these needs, and the way in which they are met, have to be viewed in relation to the development situation of the country: are the benefits of the transfer in meeting legitimate security needs greater than their cost in terms of the impact on the development of the country? Even if the legitimate security needs of a state do take precedence, is the importing government likely to abide by international human rights and humanitarian law?

Security and development: weighing the costs

Arms transfers may be essential to support a state's legitimate security needs or to improve the capacity of its security forces. Research by the World Bank also reveals that security is a main priority for poor people in all regions of the world and a necessary condition for improving their quality of life. **However, in order for arms transfers to support development, the potential security benefits must be carefully weighed alongside the wider development needs of the importing country and the human rights of its people.** The opportunity costs of some recent arms transfers underline this point.

In 2002, arms deliveries to Asia, the Middle East, Latin America, and Africa constituted 66.7 per cent of the value of all arms deliveries worldwide, with a monetary value of nearly US$17bn; the five permanent members of the United Nations Security Council accounted for 90 per cent of those deliveries. Meanwhile, across these regions:

- more than a billion people struggled to survive on less than a dollar a day;
- one child in five did not complete primary school;
- more than 14 million children lost one or both parents to AIDS in 2001;
- nearly 800 million people suffered from chronic hunger;
- half a million women died in pregnancy or childbirth.

The misue of arms can further impede development. Irresponsible arms transfers may: encourage unaccountable and poorly trained military forces to suppress human rights and democratic development; facilitate brutal resource exploitation; contribute to environmental degradation; and to an increase in violence against women. In these cases, the development needs of the country continue to go unmet, and in some situations may increase still further. Poverty may deepen, inequalities may widen, access to basic services be further compromised, and livelihoods be threatened.

Promises in pieces

The right to sustainable development is enshrined in international human rights instruments and declarations. In addition, exporter governments have made specific commitments under numerous regional and multilateral arms export-control regimes to take the impact of arms exports on importer countries' sustainable development into account when making arms licensing decisions. The 1993 Organisation for Security and Cooperation in Europe (OSCE) Principles Governing Conventional Arms Transfers, the 1998 EU Code of Conduct, the 2000 OSCE Document on Small Arms and Light Weapons, and the 2002 Wassenaar Arrangement Best Practice Guidelines for Small Arms and Light Weapons all set out the foundations for specifically taking sustainable development into account in arms transfers. **However, in too many cases exporting governments are failing to respect the commitments they have made. This is unacceptable. Exporting states urgently need to engage more fully with the impact of arms transfers on sustainable development by adopting a thorough and transparent methodology for assessment.**

Promises into practice

The development and adoption of an international Arms Trade Treaty provides the opportunity to establish such a methodology, and strengthen existing regional and multilateral export-control agreements. Article 4c of the proposed Arms Trade Treaty states that, excepting legitimate security needs, an arms transfer must not go ahead if it is likely to adversely affect sustainable development. **Research for this report has determined that the following three levels of analysis are key to the development of a methodology for making this assessment.**

- **Identify arms sales of possible concern using triggers.** Triggers should include questions that consider the significance of the financial value of the transfer and/or arms deal, in combination with a consideration of the development situation of the importer country.

- **Map the development and human security status of importing countries using indicators.** These should capture not only economic, but also social and human development characteristics by incorporating an assessment of progress in achieving the MDGs, of gender in development, and of human security.

- **Deeper context and deal-specific questioning of arms-procurement processes to make an arms-export judgement against key factors.** These should investigate responsible governance, arms-procurement decision making; import rationale and appropriateness and affordability against this justification; and importer capacity in terms of industrial and technological capability, and technical capacity.

This methodology should be agreed and implemented by all arms exporters with immediate effect, as a key tool to prevent arms being exported to where they will undermine sustainable development and divert scarce resources from fighting poverty.

Part 5 of this report sets out the proposed methodology in more detail. Its structure and rationale is based upon insights drawn from research findings presented in the report's preceding parts: the foundations of sustainable development and the significance of arms transfers in this context (Part 1); the range of impacts of arms transfers on sustainable development (Part 2); a review of current arms exporter practice vis-à-vis sustainable development (Part 3); and an investigation of key governance, security and development concerns in the importer context (Part 4).

1 Weighing the costs

Article 51 of the United Nations Charter recognises that every state has a right to individual and collective self-defence and Articles 1(3), 55 and 56 pledge member states to promote and encourage respect and observance of human rights to achieve, amongst other things, 'higher standards of living, full employment and conditions of economic and social progress and development'. Arms transfers may be essential to support a state's legitimate security needs, or to improve the capacity of its security forces that are required sometimes to use minimal armed force to stop violent criminal acts where there is a direct threat to life.[1] Research by the World Bank revealed that security was a main priority for poor people in all regions of the world, and a necessary condition for improving their quality of life. [2]

Development and arms transfers are not therefore mutually exclusive. **However, in order that arms transfers do not undermine development, they must have sustainable development and the goal of *human security* at their core. The security benefits to be derived from arms transfers must be carefully weighed alongside the wider development needs of the importing country and against exporter profit.** Article 26 of the UN Charter makes this clear, setting out the responsibility of states 'to promote the establishment and maintenance of international peace and security with the least diversion for armaments of the world's human and economic resources.'[3] **The Millennium Development Goals (MDGs) agreed in September 2000 by all 189 UN member states will not be achieved if resources are diverted from this vital task by inappropriate arms transfers.**

> 'Arms transfers' in this report covers all forms of licensed movements of arms, military equipment and components, including military aid, free gifts, commercial sales, government to government sales, and licensed production.
>
> 'Developing countries' in this report, unless otherwise specified, includes medium development and low development countries, and middle- and low-income countries.

Arms transfers to developing countries: a costly business

Throughout the 1970s, arms sales to the developing world were financed by low-interest loans. When global interest rates rose in the 1970s and 1980s, a mountain of debt impoverished many developing countries. War has plunged some of these countries even deeper into debt.

- For states such as El Salvador, Ethiopia, Mozambique, Somalia, Sri Lanka, Sudan, and Uganda, involvement in military conflict has been a major cause of indebtedness.

Crispin Hughes/Oxfam

This school bell in Adi Keshi camp for internally displaced people in Eritrea is an old Ethiopian shell.

- Of the 150 wars fought between the end of the Second World War and the mid-1990s, more than nine out of ten occurred in the developing world.[4]

- Wars also exacerbate the effects of famine and can severely impede the delivery of aid to bring relief. Examples include Chad (1984), Ethiopia (1984, 1987, and 1998), Mozambique (1984, 1987), Somalia (1984), and Sudan (1984, 1998).[5]

Although arms transfers fuel wars they do not *cause* wars, and in many cases countries that go to war may have legitimate security needs. However, the costs of meeting these needs, and the way in which they are met, have to be viewed in relation to the development situation of the country.

By 1994, it was estimated that one-fifth of the developing world's debt was due to arms imports.[6] Developing country governments continue regularly to commit huge proportions of meagre national budgets to the military. Often, the only figures available for analysis are military expenditure, which includes salaries and infrastructure costs, as well as the cost of arms imports. However, arms transfers, and the costs of maintaining and using the weapons, are a highly significant part of this expenditure in the majority of cases.

In certain developing countries, governments spend more on the military than on social development, communications infrastructure, and health combined. Even where such countries have been developing their own domestic arms industries, expenditure on arms imports is high.

Spending on health, education and the military in developing countries[7]

Seven developing countries spend more on military than on health and education *combined:*

Oman, Syria, Burma, Sudan, Pakistan, Eritrea, Burundi – see figure below.

Fourteen developing countries spend more on the military than on *both* health and education taken *individually:*

Saudi Arabia, Jordan, Turkey, Sri Lanka, Iran, Cambodia, China, Ecuador, Nigeria, Rwanda, Angola, Guinea-Bissau, Ethiopia, Sierra Leone

Twelve developing countries spend more on the military than on *either* education or health:

Macedonia, Lao, Morocco, Lebanon, Egypt, India, Armenia, Zimbabwe, Uganda, Yemen, Cameroon, Nepal

Figure 1: Developing countries spending more on military than education and health combined

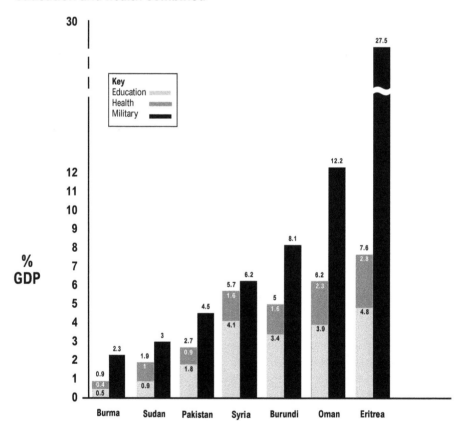

Source: Human Development Report, UNDP 2003.

Note: Figures are based on public expenditure on education from 1998–2000, or estimates from 1990 where this figure is missing; public expenditure on health in 2000, or in 1990 where this figure is missing; and military expenditure in 2001; all as a percentage of GDP. Only countries with low or medium development, as specified by the Human Development Index, are listed.

Figure 2: In 2002 the permanent five members of the UN Security Council accounted for 90 per cent of arms deliveries to the Middle East, Asia, Latin America and Africa

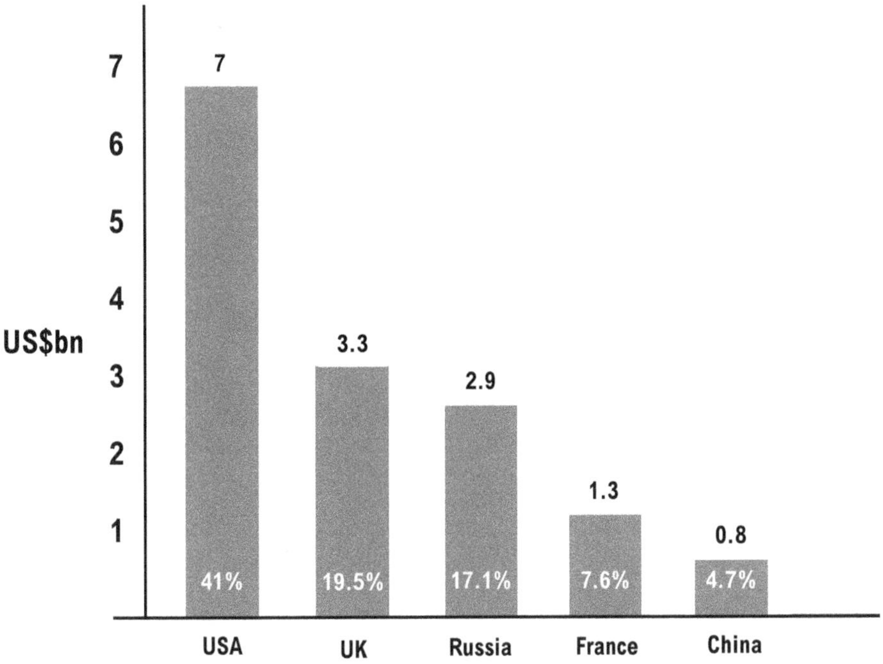

Source: CRS Report to Congress, 'Conventional Arms Transfers to Developing Nations 1995-2002', September 22 2003, R. F. Grimmett

In 2002, the permanent members of the UN Security Council – China, France, the Russian Federation, the UK and the USA – were the top five arms exporters in the world, together responsible for 88 per cent of conventional arms exports. The USA dominated the industry, contributing almost half (45 per cent) of all the world's exported weapons. **In 2002, arms deliveries to Asia, the Middle East, Latin America, and Africa constituted 66.7 per cent of the value of all arms deliveries worldwide, with a monetary value of nearly US$17bn.**[8]

As these figures illustrate, the arms market is big business, even to regions with a high proportion of developing nations. In addition, and increasingly in the wake of the 'war on terror', military aid, grants, and loans are extended to developing countries across the world. While these are in a sense 'free gifts', direct financial costs are likely to be incurred by the recipient states through the demands of maintenance, training, and infrastructure requirements.

Sustainable development: strong foundations

Sustainable development - a combination of economic growth and social progress that meets the needs of the present without compromising the ability of future generations to meet their own needs[9] **- is firmly grounded in international human rights law:**

- Articles 25 and 26 of the Universal Declaration of Human Rights agreed in 1948 underscore the rights to an adequate standard of living and education. Articles 11, 12 and 13 of the International Covenant on Economic, Social and Cultural Rights, which entered into force in 1976 elaborate these rights. [10]

- In 1986, the UN General Assembly adopted a 'Declaration on the Right to Development', stating that 'the human person is the central subject of development' and calling upon member states to 'ensure access to the basic resources, education, health services, food, housing, employment and the fair distribution of income.' Article 7 calls upon all states to 'promote the establishment, maintenance and strengthening of international peace and security' and, to that end, to 'do their utmost to achieve general and complete disarmament under effective international control as well as to ensure that the resources released by effective disarmament measures are used for comprehensive development, in particular that of the developing countries.' [11]

These rights have since been reiterated and built upon in numerous summits, resolutions, and declarations by the United Nations and also by groups of developing countries themselves, such as the Intergovernmental Authority on Development (IGAD) and the New Partnership for African Development (NEPAD), see Appendix 1.

Since 2002, the proliferation and misuse of small arms and light weapons has become an issue for the UN Human Rights Commission and the Sub-Commission on Human Rights, which have considered reports by a newly appointed Special Rapporteur on Human Rights and Small Arms. The Rapporteur has set out the international legal obligations of states to control arms.
See: Prevention of human rights violations committed with small arms and light weapons - Preliminary report submitted by Barbara Frey, Special Rapporteur, in accordance with Sub-Commission resolution 2002/25, E/CN.4/Sub.2/2002/39.

The Millennium Development Goals: promises into practice?

Over the past three decades, there has been some real progress towards achieving sustainable development: life expectancy in poor countries has increased by eight years, and illiteracy has been cut in half.[12] However, **governments have fallen far short of fulfilling the promises contained in their bold statements and commitments to sustainable development**. Oxfam reported in 2000 that 'The world's governments, including the rich and powerful G7, have comprehensively reneged on human development commitments made at a series of high profile United Nations conferences through the 1990s.'[13]

Seeking to devise a measurable framework to turn their promises into practice, 147 heads of state and government, and 189 UN Member States agreed in September 2000 to a set of time-bound and measurable goals

Jenny Matthews/Oxfam

William, from Kitovu in Uganda, was dying of AIDS, and was desperately seeking help to look after his six-year-old daughter, Maria.

By 2015, the Millennium Development Goals aim to:
1. Halve extreme poverty and hunger
2. Achieve universal primary education
3. Promote gender equality and empower women
4. Reduce child mortality
5. Improve maternal health
6. Combat HIV/AIDS, malaria, and other diseases
7. Ensure environmental sustainability
8. Develop a global partnership for development

and targets to progress towards achieving sustainable development globally by 2015. The 'Millennium Development Goals' represent a framework to tackle poverty, improve access to basic services, bring disease under control, and ensure education for all.

Critics of the MDGs cite the fact that they represent a 'lowest common denominator' in terms of commitment, and are not binding. However, **the MDGs are now seen as the main set of international commitments on which a framework for action for sustainable development is based, and provide a useful *measurable* set of targets – alongside all human rights and development commitments to date – by which to hold governments to account.** This is particularly important, since, as the United Nations Development Programme's Human Development Report stated in 2003:

- more than a billion people struggled to survive on less than a dollar a day. Most of them also lacked access to basic health services and safe drinking water;

- one child out of five did not complete primary school;

- in much of the developing world, the HIV/AIDS pandemic continued to spread unchecked. More than 14 million children lost one or both parents to the disease in 2001, and the number of AIDS orphans is expected to double by 2010;

- nearly 800 million people, or 15 per cent of the world's population, suffered from chronic hunger;

- half a million women died in pregnancy or childbirth — or one for every minute of every day. A woman in sub- Saharan Africa was 100 times more likely to die in pregnancy or childbirth than a woman in Western Europe. [14]

The MDGs and arms expenditure [15]

The countries of Africa, Latin America, Asia, and the Middle East hold 51 per cent of the world's heavy weapons.

In the Middle East and North Africa:

Since 1990, the percentage of people living on less than US$1 per day has not decreased, and the percentage living on less than US$2 per day has increased from 21 per cent to 23 per cent of the population.

This region spends an average of US$12bn per year on arms imports; more than Latin America, Africa, and Asia put together.

In sub-Saharan Africa:

The number of people living in poverty is expected to rise from 315 million in 1999 to 404 million by 2015.

HIV/AIDS is the leading cause of death in sub-Saharan Africa, but malaria and tuberculosis are also serious problems.

Life expectancy has declined from 50 years to 46 years since 1990.

In this region, military expenditure has increased steadily from 1995 to 2001, increasing by 47 per cent over this period.

In South Asia:

Nearly half of all children under the age of five are malnourished.

Youth illiteracy is high: 23 per cent for males and 39 per cent for females.

South Asia is one of only three world sub-regions where militarisation is increasing: militarisation levels doubled from 1994 to 2001 (as measured by the BIC3D index - see Chapter 3).

In Central Asia:

Countries that could no longer afford the huge social infrastructure they inherited have experienced a reversal of many social indicators, including rising infant mortality rates and deteriorating school enrolments.

In Central Asia, weapons holdings have increased by nine per cent in the last four years for which figures are available (1998 to 2001).

Governments are not doing enough to meet the MDGs by 2015. One year after the MDGs were announced, Kofi Annan said that only political will was missing,[16] and four years on, James Wolfensohn, president of the World Bank, called it a 'fundamental imbalance' that the world should spend US $900bn on defence; around US $325bn on agricultural subsidies and only US $50bn to US $60bn on aid.[17] There is no time to lose in demonstrating this will. **There is an urgent need to take stock of the shortfall between the rhetoric and reality of action around sustainable development needs worldwide, and to ensure that policies and practice do more to address this gap. The role of arms transfers is often overlooked, but as the scale and the nature of the business illustrates, it is a key part of the picture.**

Voicing concern

Concerns about the impact of arms transfers have been raised by international organisations, civil society groups, and even by importing governments themselves.[18]

International organisations

The UNDP's 1994 Human Development Report (HDR) – a landmark document that first set out the parameters of 'human security' - stated that '[a]rms spending undermines human security ... by eating up precious resources that could have been used for human development.'[19]

An arms importing spree in India

In January 2004, it was announced that the Indian Government is to finalise the purchase of a Russian-made aircraft carrier as part of a package worth around US$1.5bn. This represents the continuation of a 'military spending spree' – it is India's third big arms deal in a period of five months. If it goes through, the purchase of the *Gorshkov* will probably be the largest single defence deal that India has entered into with any country since Independence. The cost of the carrier and the aircraft is equal to the entire Indian naval budget for the past three years. Added to this will be the cost of the special infrastructure that will have to be created if the navy is to operate the ship successfully. **To put the purchase in perspective, the cost is the equivalent of that required to provide one year of antiretroviral AIDS drugs for 10 million AIDS patients.**[20]

India is the only country in the region to have an aircraft carrier. Its main neighbours, Pakistan and China, do not have them. In addition, the Indian Government's claim that the *Gorshkov* is a temporary replacement for an existing carrier that is due for decommissioning is being criticised by Indian analysts.[21]

India and Pakistan, where many people live in desperate poverty, are cases in point. **The reasons for such poverty are complex and numerous; however, their governments' large expenditures on arms and other military equipment has meant there is less money available for public health, education, and poverty reduction,** and this has not helped to lift these countries from the lowest third of nations on the United Nations' Human Development Index.

International Financial Institutions such as the World Bank also raise concerns about the possible opportunity costs of some arms transfers. The World Bank 'participated in some of the discussions' concerning the purchase by Tanzania of the 'Watchman' air traffic control system in 2001, 'given that the Air Traffic Control System (ATC) under consideration involved a large commitment of public resources and foreign borrowing.'[22] The World Bank also engaged the International Civil Aviation Organization to conduct a study of the proposed deal, a study that questioned both the military and civilian capabilities of the control system.[23]

Donors, military expenditure, and arms transfers

There is little evidence of the influence of development-aid ministries on arms-import decisions.

Research in **Ghana** suggests that aid 'conditionality' may be on the donor agenda – but this concern does not appear to extend to the level of imported weapons.

According to one **Danish** official in Ghana, 'if the [Ghanaian] government increases military expenditure by, say, 10 per cent, there will be very much concern' in Denmark. The official also noted that such an increase would be discussed among Denmark's bilateral partners in order to design a common response.

An official at the **Japanese** Embassy in Ghana argued that Japan is not influenced by Ghana's military expenditure when discussing development aid. However, Japan demands that none of its development aid is diverted for military purposes.

According to the **UK** Department for International Development representatives in Accra, it is 'part of [UK] global policy to take into account the military expenditure when discussing development aid'. They emphasised the point that the donor community is concerned with levels of military expenditure in Ghana and in all recipient countries.

Although Ghana's development partners express concern about military expenditure, none of those interviewed was categorical about Ghana's spending levels.[24]

Civil Society

Civil society groups concerned about excessive military spending frequently voice the argument that military spending occurs at the expense of social development.

- In 2001, the president of the Chilean Medical Association called for a 20 per cent cut to Chile's defence budget, claiming that this would make available US$600m for spending on health care.[25]

A peace festival in southern Senegal juxtaposes the call for peace and reconciliation ('reconciliation – paix') with army tanks.

* In Croatia, a MiG-21 upgrade project provoked public commentary. Ongoing and open media and civil society opposition to the deal and its cost in the face of much needed social development spending, bolstered a new government elected in 2000 in its decision to reduce spending on the project.

Pressure from non-government actors in South Africa

A number of observers of the South African arms trade note that South Africa desperately needs to spend money on the 'development of civil industry, water supplies, education, housing and health, above all on mitigation of the catastrophe that is AIDS', and that the defence industry diverted funds away from these development priorities.[26]

In 2001, a group of economists went further, and challenged the government's major arms-import package on constitutional grounds, noting that the South African Bill of Rights extends to the 'second generation' rights of housing, healthcare, food, and other social needs. The economists lodged a class action suit on behalf of 'the class of poor people in South Africa,' which called for the cancellation of the armaments-acquisition programme, based on arguments that it was strategically, economically, and financially irrational. The last noted that the foreign exchange and other financial risks limited the state's ability to meet the socio-economic commitments of the Bill of Rights.[27] On 4 March 2004, the case was rejected by the Cape Town High Court. The Judge stated that the challenge should have focused 'on the real and effective decision to acquire these arms, namely that of Cabinet'. The economists have stated that they will appeal the decision.[28]

Women, arms transfers, and sustainable development

Women, in particular, have become outspoken on the need to take into account the impact of arms transfers on sustainable development. It was women's groups who brought the question of military expenditure on to the agenda of the 1992 Rio Earth Summit. Principle 20 of the Rio Declaration stated, 'Women have a vital role in environmental management and development. Their full participation is therefore essential to achieve sustainable development.'

In 1995, at the Fourth UN World Conference on Women in Beijing, the Platform for Action stated that 'Excessive military expenditures, including global military expenditures and arms trade or trafficking, and investments for arms production and acquisition have reduced the resources available for social development.'[29]

Importer governments

In some cases, importer governments themselves have acknowledged the potential opportunity cost of arms spending on sustainable development.

The recognition by the new Croatian government in 2000 that military spending in general – and the proposed US$120m upgrade of 12 MiG-21 planes in particular – would divert funds from pressing social programmes was an implicit acknowledgement of the opportunity cost of arms procurement for sustainable development. The final contract, in 2001, of US$8.5m to overhaul eight MiG-21 aircraft and to import four Romanian trainer aircraft was of 'relatively small value [and] precluded interdepartmental feuds over funds'.[30]

Similarly, in January 2003, Brazil's new government under President Lula decided to suspend the purchase of 12 military jets costing between US$700m and US$1bn, reportedly so that it could spend more on social programmes. About 15 per cent of the country's population are seriously malnourished, and around 33 per cent of all Brazilians live in poverty.[31]

The need for engagement

Finding an effective way for exporting governments to control arms transfers according to, among other considerations, a specific assessment of their impact on sustainable development is crucial for poor countries. As well as Article 26 of the UN Charter, the basic responsibility of all states – importer and exporter – is established under the International Covenant on Economic, Social and Cultural Rights to contribute to the progressive realisation of these rights through international assistance and co-operation. The Declaration on the Right to Development also recognises a collective international obligation to promote development, and requires states to 'cooperate with each other in ensuring development and eliminating obstacles to development.'[32]

Several agreements in multilateral fora – the Organisation for Security and Cooperation in Europe (OSCE), Wassenaar Arrangement, European Union – require participating states to take sustainable development into account *specifically in arms transfers.*

However, research for this report has shown that most have little real commitment to implement the principle. **Exporting states need to engage more fully with, and weigh more carefully, the impact of arms transfers on sustainable development alongside concerns of security and against profit, by adopting a thorough and transparent methodology for assessment.**

The Arms Trade Treaty

The development and adoption of an international Arms Trade Treaty (ATT) provides the opportunity to work towards the establishment of such a methodology. The Arms Trade Treaty proposed by Oxfam, Amnesty International, the Arias Foundation, Project Ploughshares, Saferworld, the Federation of American Scientists and other NGOs in the International Action Network on Small Arms focuses on the supply of arms, and once adopted, will be an international means of control to ensure that all nations are working to the same standard of arms transfers (see Appendix 2). This Treaty will also help to ensure that deals rejected by one exporter are not licensed or authorised by another.

Article 4 of the proposed Treaty lists several factors which must be considered when making an export decision, and Article 4c clearly states that an arms transfer must not go ahead if it is likely to adversely affect sustainable development. At the time of writing, the ATT text is still under development by a group of international legal experts and policy makers – the current text reads as follows:

> *In considering whether any international transfer of arms may be authorised ... Contracting Parties shall take into account whether transfers of arms of the kind under consideration are likely to adversely affect sustainable development ... In such a circumstance there shall be a presumption against authorisation.*[33]

The research undertaken for this report has provided a basis for considering how this may be done. Building on the insights from the key findings in chapters 2–4, a suggested framework methodology is presented in chapter 5.

2 Causes for concern: the impacts of arms transfers on sustainable development

There are several areas in which arms transfers can impact negatively on sustainable development:

- the financial opportunity costs of arms transfers in terms of increasing social development;

- the impact of arms transfers on economic growth;

- the effects of the misuse of arms;

- and the cumulative impact of arms transfers on all of the above.

These impacts are inter-related, and have immediate, medium- and long-term consequences that are dependent on the nature of the transfer, and on the social, political, and economic context of the country in question. However, the consequences are also not always clear-cut, and have to be weighed alongside the legitimate security needs of the country and respect for international human rights standards in the governance of its people. **There is a need to develop an assessment methodology that elucidates both the potential negative impact of transfers and the possibility that in some cases their impact may be either positive or an unavoidable cost.**

> **Research methodology: literature review**
>
> This chapter is based on research undertaken for a literature review by Project Ploughshares.[34] The review involved the survey of literature from the fields of economics, international relations, and development studies, in order to determine if there exists a common understanding of the impact of arms transfers on development.
>
> While much of the research surveyed is based on military expenditure rather than on arms transfers *per se*, due to the paucity of research on the latter, arms transfers are a highly significant part of military expenditure, and the arguments remain valid in this context.
>
> This chapter also draws on original research, and secondary research conducted for nine case studies (presented in more detail in chapter 4).

Opportunity Costs

The most obvious and immediate impact arises from the monetary cost of the transfer itself. The cost of arms imports must usually be found from the government budget. Developing countries generally spend a *greater proportion* of their national product on arms than do rich countries.[35] In recent years:

- nearly half of the countries with the highest defence burden had low indicators of human development;[36]

- Indonesia, the second highest recipient of overseas aid, spent almost the same sum of money on its military forces as it received in aid;[37]

- Pakistan's total defence expenditures consumed one third of its gross domestic product. With the servicing of debt on loans to finance foreign arms purchases, this figure rose to 50 per cent.[38]

While a diversion of resources from social spending to military spending cannot be assumed (and vice versa), it has occurred in some circumstances.[39] In such cases, military purchases result in cuts in public expenditures on health, education, and other basic services.[40] **Since the early 1990s, the World Bank has recognised the opportunity costs of military spending, and concluded that military expenditure may divert resources from the development programme of some borrowers.**[41]

The development cost of arms transfers in South Africa

In 1999, South Africa agreed to purchase armaments – including frigates, submarines, aircraft, and helicopters – at a cost of the equivalent of R36bn (US$6bn) in 2003 from suppliers including Germany, France, Sweden, and the UK. This spending is far in excess of that on some other projects of the government:

- extending old-age payout systems to children: slightly more than R1bn (US$166.6m) a year;
- land restitution: R550m (US$91.6m) a year;
- combating HIV/AIDS: R323m (US$53.8m) a year.

All of these are vitally important projects, which were introduced in addition to normal state running costs. In other words, they constitute the real discretionary spend of the government. The cost of these entire projects together still totals less than the sum that the government pays every year to foreign companies for arms.[42] **The six billion dollars could have purchased treatment with combination therapy for all five million AIDS sufferers for two years.**[43]

Most recently, the opportunity cost of spending on arms was starkly illustrated in India and Pakistan.

- When India signed a contract to buy a US$1bn military radar system in October 2003, foreign aid agencies were still searching for US$50m in donations to defeat the country's polio epidemic.

- The same year in Pakistan, armed forces were updating their multibillion-dollar shopping list, including a request for US-made F-16 jets, while aid groups fighting a tuberculosis epidemic struggled to fill a lethal funding gap. Tuberculosis kills more than 50,000 Pakistanis a year, and infects 250,000.

Both polio and tuberculosis could be eradicated if adequate vaccination programmes were funded.[44] In recent years, the Indian government has made a string of major arms imports (see table on page 21) despite the fact that, according to the government's own figures, barely 50 per cent of India's adult population is literate, almost 200 million lack access to clean water, and more than 300 million have to survive on less than 50 cents per day.

A peaceful use for a tank in a park in Hyderabad, India.

Table 1: The development costs of arms procurement in India

Weapons imports	Amount in US Dollars	Other options in US Dollars
Sukhoi-30 MKI fighter aircraft from Russia (deal agreed and 32 ordered in 2000) Source : http://news.bbc.co.uk/2/low/business/2479781.stm	$1.8bn	One extra year of primary schooling for 20 million girls ($85 per year per child)
Submarines: technical negotiations have been underway with French consortium DCN-CSF Thomson (now THALES/DCNI) since 2001 for acquiring 6 Scorpene Class (Project 75) submarines for Navy Source : www.bharat-rakshak.com/NAVY/Project75.html; *the Financial Express* www.financialexpress.com/fe_full_story. php?content_id=47958; *the Tribune,* www.tribuneindia.com/2002/20021012/main5.htm	$1.8bn	Three years of treatment for 1.7 billion children suffering from debilitating intestinal worms ($0.35 per child per year) Figures based on 2004 costs for drugs, one full treatment per year.
Battle tanks: 310 T-90S Main Battle Tanks (MBT) from Russia, (deal signed in 2001, 124 tanks delivered. Balance of 186 tanks to be manufactured in India under licence.) Source: www.biiss.org/nuclear/Feb2001/08.htm	$600m	200 million insecticide-treated nets for beds to reduce malaria mortality ($3 per net) Source: www.psi.org/resources/pubs/imns.html
Aircraft: 10 Mirage-2000E FGA aircraft from France, (ordered in 2000) Source: SIPRI, http://projects.sipri.se/armstrade/INDIA_MPTS_93-02.pdf	$325m	The prevention of a multitude of vitamin and mineral deficiencies by adding essential vitamins and minerals to foods (such as flour, salt, sugar, cooking oil and margarine) that are regularly consumed by most people for more than one billion people over a ten-year period. ($0.03 per person per year) Source: UNICEF 2004
Aircraft: 5 Legacy corporate jets for Air Force from Brazilian aircraft maker Embraer (ordered in 2003) Source:www.rediff.com/money/2003/sep/19jets.htm	$88m	One year's basic rural water and sanitation services for 6 million people in developing countries ($14.50 per person)
Hawk fighter jets from Britain's BAE (66 ordered in 2002) Source : *Frontline,* 20 (20), September 27–October 10 2003 www.spacewar.com/2004/040319144251.2k85vojx.html	$1.7bn	One year of antiretroviral AIDS drugs for more than 11 million AIDS patients ($150 per year per patient) For costings, see: www.accessmed-msf.org/campaign/faq.shtm and www.accessmed-msf.org/prod/publications.asp?scntid=22420041625454&contenttype=PARA&
Admiral Gorshkov aircraft carrier from Russia (deal signed 2004) Source: The *Hindu,* 21 January 2004 www.hindu.com/2004/01/21/stories/2004012105940100.htm	$1.5bn	Basic survival income for one year for 1.1 million families ($120 per family per month)

Data Compiled by A.W. Dorn and B. Nepram, February 2004. Where no source is given, the per-person expenditures on social programmes are taken from a table in R. Leger Sivard, *World Military and Social Expenditure* (Washington, DC: World Priorities, 1996). These figures are estimates for the developing world.

The purchase by Tanzania of the US$40m Watchman radar system from the UK in 2001 was, according to experts, vastly too expensive and inappropriate for its use,[45] and an unsuitable use of money in a country in which 46 per cent of the population are undernourished. **US$ 40m could have provided healthcare for 3.5 million people in Tanzania.**

Tanzania's MDG Country Report states that it is unlikely to meet the Millennium targets on hunger, education, reproductive health, and under-five mortality, and will only potentially fulfil targets on poverty, HIV/AIDS, and the environment.

Opportunity costs in the context of the Millennium Development Goals

An average of US$22bn a year is spent on arms by countries in Africa, Asia, the Middle East, and Latin America – a sum that would have enabled those countries to be on track to meet the Millennium Development Goals of achieving universal primary education and targets for reducing infant and maternal mortality (estimated cost US$10bn and US$12bn respectively).[46] While in some cases, spending on arms is required to meet legitimate security needs – needs which themselves can support development – the contrast between readily acquiring arms and spending directly on development needs is stark in much of the world.

Opportunity costs for gender equality

Experience has shown that in many cases it is women and girls who feel the most immediate consequences of cuts in social services, because they are often responsible for the family's well being.[47] If there is no well near the village, women walk long distances to fetch water; if there are inadequate ante- and post-natal services, their health, and that of their baby, will be compromised; and it is generally young girls who are the lowest priority when it comes to attending school.

Women also have different and unequal opportunities for the protection, promotion, and maintenance of their health. These include unequal access to basic health services, disproportionate responsibilities in the family and society, discrimination and experiences of violence, and unsafe pregnancies.[48]

'Hidden' financial costs

The financial costs of arms transfers are not always immediately apparent. In late 1999, the US government agreed to give Ghana two inshore patrol vessels to ensure that no other state was encroaching on Ghana's fishing waters – a legitimate justification that clearly seeks to support sustainable development and the livelihoods of Ghana's fishing communities (see discussion later in this chapter). Although these boats were virtually free, they are thought to be costing the Ghanaian Government about US$1m a year each in up-keep and maintenance, costs that were apparently not discussed or assessed at the time of their transfer.[49]

Sewerage and drainage is a major public health problem in cities in developing countries around the world. Here in Accra, Ghana, the sewers overflowed in 1995, leading to loss of life and destruction of property.

Imported arms may therefore be cheap to buy or even free, but may in the medium and long term involve significant infrastructure, maintenance, personnel, and spare-part costs. Military assistance is of particular concern in this regard. Military-assistance programmes have increased considerably in the context of the 'war on terror'.

US spending priorities: military assistance and the 'war on terror'

For 2004, the US State Department set aside US$4.7bn for counter-terrorism, compared with US$2bn for programmes for the war against poverty. The amount includes military assistance to the so-called 'frontline states', a group of 25 countries that includes the Philippines, Afghanistan, and Yemen, nations that support the current US counter-terrorism campaign. The aid will arrive in the form of military services, equipment, and training.

In 2005, US President Bush is proposing to increase funding for his two key anti-poverty initiatives, the Millennium Challenge Account and funds to fight HIV/AIDS for African and Caribbean countries, but he is also cutting funds to other key humanitarian and development accounts. He is also asking Congress to increase military and security assistance by more than US$1bn, particularly to the aforementioned 'frontline' states.

Under President Bush's proposals, credits for foreign militaries to buy US weapons and equipment would increase by some US$700m to nearly US$5bn, the highest total in well over a decade. US military spending – which already constitutes roughly half of the world's total military expenditure – would rise by some seven per cent, to US$402bn. It should be noted that these figures also include funds for US donor commitments and debt-reduction support for Afghanistan and Iraq.

To accommodate the big increases in defence and homeland security, the overall budget proposes significant domestic cuts to agriculture, transportation, and environmental protection, among other non-security-related items.[50]

The fact that arms transfers involve these costs does not necessarily make them unjustifiable, but **for all transfers, an accurate assessment of costs should be made prior to agreement, including costs of maintenance and overhaul of equipment; training of staff for its use; infrastructure; and long-term management costs. The exporter should help the importer to make this assessment.**[51]

In addition, the true economic costs of arms imports are often concealed through off-budget purchases, and are therefore not apparent in government accounts.

Economic growth

In the medium to long term, military spending can distort the economies of developing countries, diverting scarce financial resources and trained personnel from projects that could create wealth and benefit the poor.

- Conflict in northern Uganda is costing the Ugandan economy at least US$100m every year, according to research conducted by civil society organisations. [52] This is clearly an amount that the country cannot afford to lose.

- **A survey examining military expenditures in 125 nations between 1972 and 1988 found that, for many nations, military spending occurred at the expense of economic and social development, resulting in a lower rate of economic growth.**[53]

- Other studies suggest that the military tends to attract limited human and other resources away from the civilian industrial sector.[54]

- Governments may also increase military spending by borrowing foreign exchange, which can lead to higher levels of debt.[55]

Geoff Sayer/Oxfam

Boy carrying water back to his family's temporary home in a displaced camp in western Uganda. There are 1.6 million internally displaced people in Uganda[i], and an estimated 25 million in the world[ii].
i   World Food Programme, 19 April 2004, CAP 2004 Revision proposal
ii UNHCR, Refugees by Numbers, 2003.

It is important to point out that some research has found that there is no general evidence that military spending tends to restrict investment in developing countries.[56] Indeed, the ambiguity of data and anecdotal evidence that characterises research into the relationship between economic growth and arms transfers is an indication of the complexity of this relationship, and the need for case-by-case analyses.[57]

The misuse of arms

Weapons in the wrong hands have acute, immediate impacts on personal, economic, social, and civil rights, which translate into longer-term effects that prevent development.[58]

Denial of freedoms

Irresponsible arms transfers may encourage unaccountable and poorly trained military forces to deny human rights and suppress democratic development.[59] While stronger military and police forces may provide better security (see discussion below), research has shown that transfers to *military regimes* are more likely to serve the interests of the regimes than those of human development and security. [60]

For example, the abuse and proliferation of small arms is often characteristic of suppression of pressure for democratic change. The threatening use of such arms by security forces, armed groups, or others in positions of authority against political activists, journalists, trade unionists, and peaceful demonstrators has been well-documented for a number of developing countries, as well as for some developed countries.[61]

Destruction of lives, infrastructure, and economic opportunities

The impact on sustainable development may also be felt in terms of the direct destruction of lives and infrastructure. The most obvious cost to social development is the destruction of lives and property. As well as the real human cost of misery, injury and death, there is also the economic cost of the loss of human life, destruction of property, and economic activity foregone.[62]

The persistent misuse of arms by law enforcement agencies, particularly the police and paramilitaries, encouraged by the ability to secure further supplies of arms, can itself be a significant contributing factor in undermining development, because economic actors lose confidence in the justice sector. Where small arms are widely misused, potential business investors may well look elsewhere for a more secure environment in which to invest their capital.

Small arms and sustainable development

The impact of the misuse of small arms is felt across the world, but most keenly in poor countries. In these countries, the infrastructure required to cope with the impact of their misuse is often stretched to the limit, and the consequences for the victims' families is devastating.

According to the World Health Organization:

'Global data on the impact of small arms on the health of individuals are far from complete. However, what data are available suggest that hundreds of thousands of people are killed each year by these weapons. Millions more survive their injuries but are left with permanent physical disabilities and mental health problems. Often, victims of small arms injuries need expensive, time-consuming surgery, followed by weeks and even months of hospital treatment and rehabilitation. In many countries, this is a serious drain on the resources of poor people and already-impoverished health systems.

The situation is even more desperate for victims in "gun-rich, resource-poor" areas, where few have ready access to adequate health services. The health consequences of small arms go beyond the physical effects of an injury. The capacity for working can be destroyed, placing a major burden on families and wider social support systems. When the affected individuals are poor, the costs and tensions resulting from changed economic circumstances can lead to the disintegration of the family or the generation of more violence within it. It is clear that the scale of small arms death and injury, and their concomitant impact on societies, is huge.' [63]

Brutal resource exploitation

Arms can also become a lethal factor in securing natural resources for some rather than using them for the benefit of all. In these cases, the human security and livelihoods of those living in resource-rich areas are jeopardised. The situation in Sudan is particularly tragic, as the discovery of oil that should have brought prosperity to the country's people has instead been used to undermine development further.

Sudan's military budget has more than doubled since construction began on the Red Sea pipeline in 1998, rising from US$94.5m in 1997 to US$327m in 2000. For a country as poor as Sudan, this is a huge amount. Profits from oil exports are estimated at approximately US$400m a year, enough to pay the costs of the war in the year 2000. Shipments of weapons have arrived regularly in Sudan – mainly from China and Eastern Europe.[64]

Parallel examples are to be found in many parts of the world: the extraction of diamonds in Angola and Sierra Leone; oil in Angola; copper in Papua New Guinea; timber in Cambodia and Liberia; coltan, gold, and other minerals in the Democratic Republic of Congo (DRC). These resources have been exploited and traded by governments, armed opposition, and local military commanders in exchange for military supplies and personal financial gain. As Oxfam and Amnesty International reported in 2003, a desperate government

This mortar was found in fields outside Malanje, Angola. Until cleared in a de-mining operation, such unexploded ordnance prevented people from earning a living from farming.

will sometimes mortgage its country's future stores of precious natural resources in order to raise immediate finances to obtain weapons and ammunition.[65] **The diversion of resource wealth to weapons imports therefore represents a special case of opportunity costs.**

Environmental degradation

Following such brutal policies of resource exploitation often results in severe environmental degradation. Resource exploitation, the demand for arms, and environmental destruction form a vicious circle.

Logging and arms in Liberia

In 2001, a UN report highlighted the key role played by the logging industry in Liberia in assisting arms trafficking. The destructive logging in Liberia not only provided funds to support the war, it has also jeopardised the future ecological integrity of this critically threatened rainforest habitat. Liberia's forests are a vital part of the Upper Guinean Forest, one of the most threatened biodiversity hotspots in the world. These forests are the only home left for the highly endangered pygmy hippopotamus, and are the last stronghold in West Africa for forest elephants. In the last decades, the destruction of the rainforest in West Africa has been severe. The UN imposed timber sanctions on Liberia on 7 July 2003, in accordance with resolution 1478 (2003).[66]

Environmental degradation has also been a feature of resource extraction in Sudan. In these cases, the implications for future generations are severe. Clearly, in these situations no thought has been given to the central tenet of sustainable development: that of meeting the needs of the present without compromising the ability of future generations to meet their own needs.

Collecting water in the densely populated neighbourhood of Clara town in Liberia. More than one million people – 32% of Liberia's population – do not have access to clean, safe drinking water. Less than 30% of people in Liberia have access to latrines.
Source: 'Liberia: Water and Sanitation Problems Massive' – WHO 2003

Violence against women

In the few places where gender-disaggregated studies of firearms-related violence are being conducted, the evidence is growing that guns play a significant part in the perpetration of violence against women.[67] Armed sexual violence is horrifically widespread in heavily armed environments. Weapons can be used to facilitate rape: women and girls are raped at gunpoint while away from home collecting firewood and water, for example, or when undertaking other daily tasks. They are also vulnerable in jail or in refugee camps, where there is no place for them to hide.[68]

In non-conflict situations, a number of studies – from the USA to South Africa – have suggested that the risk of being murdered by an intimate partner increases with the availability of firearms.[69] Violence in the home by intimate partners and friends, sometimes armed, increases during conflict, as sanctions against men's violence break down, and women's social and economic vulnerability increases.[70]

Violent conflicts accelerate the process whereby women often become the sole managers of households, sole parents, and carers for elderly or injured combatants. In the midst of violent conflict and collapse, the role of women in preserving social order is crucial. Notwith-standing the importance of their roles and tasks, women's priorities in countries suffering from armed violence continue to be largely marginalised. In general, violence against women in all its forms is still pervasive and under-reported.[71]

The risk of arms races: the cumulative impact of arms transfers

The cumulative impact of arms spending is also a cause for concern, particularly in the context of arms races. Research shows that states respond in kind to military spending by their neighbours – even non-hostile ones.[72]**Arms races in the context of developing countries can have particularly severe consequences for government spending allocations**. Reacting to the Chilean government's decision to purchase F-16 jets from the USA in December 2001, a number of arms-control experts and Latin American specialists expressed concern that the purchase would 'spur a new arms race that could divert scarce public resources from badly needed butter to guns'.[73]

Irresponsible US exports into South America

In the late 1990s, after considerable pressure by industry, the US government revoked its commitment not to supply advanced weaponry into Latin America. In January 2002, the **Chilean government** announced that it had agreed to purchase ten F-16 fighter jets and related equipment for US$636m. Less than four months later, US government officials declared that they would permit the sale to Brazil of another advanced weapon: the AIM-120 advanced medium-range air-to-air missile (AMRAAM). By making these decisions, the US government showed its disregard for the risk of a regional arms build-up and the diversion of scarce resources from pressing social needs that this new military spending will entail.

The government of Chile quickly came under criticism both at home and abroad, largely because new fighter jets were considered an unnecessary expense for a developing nation. Chilean NGOs, legislators, and even the President's own political party condemned the proposed purchase. Several regional powers, Peru being the most vocal, also called on Chile to forgo the purchase, claiming that the advanced aircraft would upset the regional military balance.

In September 2001, Peruvian Defence Minister David Waisman issued a dramatic offer to both refrain from upgrading Peru's MiG fleet and to give up their controversial Adder missiles, if Chile would agree not to buy the fighters. Chilean President Lagos summarily dismissed the offer. Lockheed's dollar-for-dollar offset package, which includes a General Electric Plant which will provide technical assistance and maintenance for the GE motors installed in the F-16s, undoubtedly made the purchase more attractive. Neither Chile nor Brazil faces any serious short-term external security threats, and even credible theoretical threats are difficult to identify.[74]

Once locked into an arms race, arms purchases will not just be one-off occurrences: increasing national and regional government resources are poured into importing arms, resources that could have been spent in addressing critical development needs.

According to one report, **India's** federal budget shows that defence spending increased by at least 14 per cent in 2003 to well over US$13bn, such that the military consumed about 15 per cent of Indian government money compared to 7 per cent which went to social services such as schools and healthcare. **Pakistan's** economy is much smaller and weaker, and more vulnerable to the costs of an arms race. Pakistan has not been able to keep up with the Indian military's spending increases. The government says it spent more than US$2.5bn on defence in 2003, which is roughly the same as in 2002.[75]

The priorities and realities of importer-government spending

Decreases in military spending will not necessarily translate into higher levels of social spending. A government's allocation of resources depends on public policy and government spending priorities.[76] Anti-democratic, highly militarised governments are more likely to expend resources on the military at the expense of development spending. However, this reality does not weaken the need to refuse exports to countries where there is a negative impact on sustainable development that cannot be justified in terms of legitimate security needs, or weaken the argument that a government *could*, where circumstances allow, allocate spending differently. Rather, it challenges policy makers to think imaginatively about how to engage with importer governments to change their spending priorities in line with the country's most pressing development needs.

For example, the IMF has introduced limits on military expenditure levels since the end of the Cold War, but so far, few savings from military budgets find their way into development priorities, as the IMF insists on redirecting them towards debt service, (although the poorest countries – Highly Indebted Poor Countries, or HIPC – are exempt from debt servicing). The OECD has argued for the reallocation of military savings to sustainable development goals.[77]

Arms-transfer deals may also tie a developing country government into a longer-term commitment, or be linked to other spending or to aid deals which could prevent them from social spending even if they wanted to do so.

Identifying the positive impact of arms transfers

The provision of security, offsets, transfers of technology and industrialisation, and the generation of taxes and employment that are associated with some arms transfers means that there are positive development gains to be derived in some circumstances, most clearly with regard to the provision of security.

The military as providers of security

Development cannot be sustained in an insecure environment. On the basis of this conclusion, the security forces do have an indirect role in sustainable development. The military may legitimately provide security from armed attacks directed against the state, and may even serve as back-up to law enforcement agencies who are required sometimes to use minimal armed force to stop violent criminal acts where there is a direct threat to life.[78] Where such security services are provided lawfully according to international standards, as set out in international human rights and humanitarian law, they can facilitate good governance, support human security, and hence help attract foreign investment, especially from foreign powers with an interest in the region, all of which can be beneficial to trade, investment, and aid.[79]

At the DFID Symposium on security-sector reform and military expenditure held in June 2000, the link between a competent military, security, and development was made clear: 'a well-run and well-governed military and other security forces are an essential support for development.'[80] The word 'competent' here is key, however, and means that **arms transfers should *only* be allowed to countries where *competent* armed forces and law enforcement agencies are trained and accountable to uphold international human rights and humanitarian law, and therefore do not deliberately abuse or violently repress civilians**.

Arms transfers and internal stability

According to the World Bank, military spending does not have a significant deterrent effect on internal rebellion, but does reduce economic growth:

'... military expenditure significantly reduces [economic] growth, while we find that [economic] growth reduces the risk of rebellion ... .'

'... military expenditure is completely insignificant in explaining **rebellion** ... although governments increase military spending in an effort to deter rebellion, the expenditure appears to be ineffective. Evidently, once a war has developed, military spending can influence its outcome, but during the inception stage of rebellion a large military response might be ineffective, or even counterproductive: excessive repression by government forces assists rebel recruitment and appears to be a common error of counter-insurgency. Indirectly, military spending might even inadvertently increase the risk of conflict through its adverse effect on economic growth.'[81]

Arms transfers to address sustainable development needs

Arms transfers can directly and positively affect sustainable development when the government has designed the import with a view to meet a specific development target. **In the case of Ghana, the research findings point to a direct and apparently positive impact on sustainable development of one very specific arms import.** The Ghanaian government's decision to acquire US naval vessels enabled the protection of fishing grounds under external threat, and resulted in fines on foreign vessels that contributed to the government treasury.[82]

Improving food sufficiency in Ghana

The acquisition of two naval depot vessels formed part of the larger Medium-term Agricultural Development Programme, initiated in 1990 to restore incentives aimed at improving food sufficiency between 50 per cent and 80 per cent. One of the identified areas for such self-sufficiency was in fisheries.[83] These programmes were also part of the larger structural adjustment programmes put in place by the administration.

A formal approach was made to the US government through the embassy in Accra after which vessels in the Defence Excess Assets programme were examined.[84] Small coastal vessels suitable for inshore patrols and larger ones for offshore patrols were subsequently delivered and used to patrol the coast.

In parliamentary discussions in 2001, the sector minister said, 'The imposition of fines on vessels arrested by our navy for illegal fishing in our maritime zone has not only helped the nation earn foreign exchange, but it has also helped to conserve our fish stocks and prevent the dumping of toxic wastes in our maritime zones ...'[85]

In one example of the key economic role that these depot vessels have played, three Spanish commercial fishing vessels that were arrested were fined the sum of US$1.4m.[86]

Offsets: the promise of future investments

Offsets, the promise of future investments as an inducement to trade, are prohibited for civil trade transactions under the World Trade Organisation (WTO) rules. However, the armaments industry has negotiated an exemption for itself on the basis of 'national security'. **Politicians frequently cite offsets to justify heavy expenditures on armaments, although experience has shown that the full promised benefits rarely materialise.** The overwhelming majority of research illustrates that offsets:

- increase rather than decrease the costs of weapons acquisition;
- distort market forces;
- can cause weapons proliferation;
- are almost impossible to monitor;
- are notorious for involving corruption;
- impede, rather than contribute to economic development.[87]

- In Saudi Arabia, the Al Yamamah arms deal was supposed to create 75,000 jobs inside Saudi Arabia. Now that the contracts are complete, it transpires that only 1,600 jobs resulted, of which 1,300 were for expatriates and only 300 for Saudi Arabians.[88]

- The South African government's decision to enter into the 1999 US$6bn arms deal with German, British, French, and Swedish companies was predicated upon the purchases being 'affordable' through offsets of foreign investments and exports intended to create 64,165 jobs. Research has since concluded that it is extremely unlikely that this number of jobs will be created. **An equivalent investment by South Africa in, for example, water supplies would have provided far more employment and other practical benefits for the poorest strata of the population.**[89]

Breakfast at Kititimo Centre for street children in Tanzania.

- At the time that the Watchman air traffic control deal was announced in Tanzania, the Tanzanian government spoke of collecting revenue from over-flight fees, and the possibility of increased tourism in a perceivably more secure environment. While there is some evidence that more aircraft have been attracted to land and re-fuel at Tanzania's airport and a number of airline companies are now looking to launch schedule and charter flights to Tanzania, this does not justify the purchase of such an expensive system.[90]

The possible positive effects of licensed production

When an agreement is reached that the weapons assembly or production will take place in the importing country – known as 'licensed production' – two areas are regularly cited as bearing positive rewards for arms importing countries: transfers of technology and the industrialisation that it entails, and the generation of taxes and employment.

It is worth noting that licensed production deals can facilitate the supply of arms to irresponsible states – there have been numerous cases of arms being sold from the licensed producer to a third country, which would not have been authorised by the original exporting state. [91]

Transfer of technology and industrialisation

Technology transfers can play a central role in building the indigenous arms-production capacity of recipient countries,[92] or increasing a firm's competitiveness and quality.[93] However, research has shown that in many cases technology transfers:

- do not provide sufficient physical, human, or technological capital to develop or sustain an indigenous arms-production capacity;[94]

- may contribute to the proliferation of weapons: transfers may increase the number of countries capable of manufacturing certain weapons in spite of licensing regimes;[95]

- where sufficient technological and human capital does exist for technology sharing, may end up becoming an argument that the industry and armed services use to push for the next generation of equipment sooner than they otherwise would, which, according to one researcher, 'is costly for taxpayers and contributes to an unnecessary arms race among allies'.[96]

In addition, **developing nations are the most unlikely group to benefit from transfers of technology**. One researcher concludes, 'As a group, developing nations do not possess the requisite capital, neither to engage in arms production nor arms co-production, and technology transfer and training do not transfer this capital in a self-sustaining matter. These capabilities apparently cannot be imported; they need to be grown indigenously.'[97]

In a related argument, some proponents of arms exports claim that military industrialisation has great benefits for its civilian counterparts. However, in most cases, research just does not support this argument.

- Military industrialisation does not generally lead to civilian industrialisation; civilian industrialisation is actually a precondition for military industrialisation.[98]

- Investment in arms production tends to replace civilian investment, and investment in military production will stimulate the civilian economy less than investment in civilian production.[99]

- The skills gained in the military sector may not be transferable to the civilian context.[100]

The generation of taxes and employment

Some research indicates that an indigenous arms-production capacity can be used to generate taxes for the state and to build foreign-exchange earnings.[101] However, there is insufficient evidence to suggest that a developing country exporting arms earns *net* foreign exchange. Research does not take into account the foreign-exchange costs of domestic arms production including, for example, the acquisition and maintenance of production capital as well as the costs of offset agreements.[102]

Others argue that the arms industry provides much needed employment and mobilises unused resources.[103] In situations of demand shortages, military spending can even increase demand for output.[104] However, while the industry creates employment opportunities for a country's most highly skilled professionals, the employment benefits of the arms industry tend not to be accessible to the poorest populations in developing countries. In addition, arms production tends to be capital-intensive, not labour-intensive. One report concludes that, 'defence production is not an effective way of dealing with problems of unemployment and/or underemployment' – a point already made with regard to offsets.[105]

The indigenisation of arms procurement in India: making up for lost time

Several years ago, the Indian government announced a self-reliance initiative which aims to increase the level of arms procurement inside India from 30 per cent to 70 per cent by 2005. Ten committees have been set up under the Department of Defence Production to identify the scope for indigenisation of items such as aircraft, electronics, and armaments. As a result, India has started to procure licences to make weapons or for other defence needs from other countries, and in May 2001, the Indian government opened its monopolistic state-owned defence industry to private participation. A foreign direct-investment limit of 26 per cent was set, in a bid to reduce the increasing dependency on imports, facilitate technology transfers, and to meet challenges posed by the digitalisation of the military hardware.[106] The Indian government's decision to privatise defence contractors came after much lobbying from Confederation of Indian Industries and several service chiefs of staff for decreased dependency on India's 39 ordnance factories and eight public-sector units.

However, this process of indigenisation has not resulted in a decrease in military spending on arms imports: not only is more money being spent on indigenous production, but also, and simultaneously, on very costly imports.[107]

3 Promises in pieces: sustainable development and arms exports

Too few governments consider sustainable development when licensing arms transfers. If the potential impact is considered at all, it is generally in such a subjective and *ad hoc* way, that at present it is difficult to account for the decisions that are taken. While the final decision as to whether or not to issue an export licence will always remain a matter of judgement, it is essential that such judgements are rooted in a thorough and transparent assessment process. **Without an agreed and publicly accessible assessment methodology, too large a part of the decision-making process relies on the – generally unaccountable – opinion of those processing the information.** If exporter governments are serious about their promises to improve sustainable development – as they have said they are, by committing themselves to the MDGs – they must act now to work towards establishing such a methodology.

Research methodology for reviewing current exporter practice
The research for this part of the report was undertaken by Saferworld, from September to December 2003.[108]The aim of the research was to provide a review of current practice in a selection of arms-export control regimes, by assessing how and where the potential impact of an arms export on sustainable development is included in arms-export authorisations. The research surveyed official policy on sustainable development, and examined how this policy is brought into legislative or procedural guidelines at the national level.

Twenty-two countries responded to the survey. From these countries, three were selected for a more in-depth study (Poland, the UK, and the USA), on the basis of reflecting a range of experiences relating to the key issues addressed in the report, and the availability of and access to information. The research used both primary and secondary sources. Government officials were approached with an initial questionnaire, and a number of interviews were also conducted. Secondary desk research was undertaken to attempt to fill in any data gaps.

Respecting regional and multilateral arrangements

Many governments have made a commitment under numerous regional and multilateral arms-export control regimes to take the impact of arms exports on importer countries' sustainable development into account when making arms licensing decisions. The 1993 Organisation for Security and Cooperation in Europe (OSCE) Principles Governing Conventional Arms Transfers (an agreement covering most major exporter states), the 1998 European Union (EU) Code of Conduct, the 2000 OSCE Document on Small Arms and Light Weapons, and the 2002 Wassenaar Arrangement Best Practice Guidelines for Small Arms and Light Weapons, all set out the foundations for specifically taking sustainable development into account in *arms transfers*.

However, the survey of arms-exporting states revealed that many of these states are failing to respect the commitments they have made:

- Two of the world's biggest arms exporters, including to developing countries – Russia, an OSCE member, and China – do not incorporate sustainable development considerations into their arms-export licensing regimes.

- Of 17 countries surveyed who are parties to the EU Code of Conduct and/or the OSCE Document:

  - only 10 would even consider denying a licence on sustainable development grounds;

  - only seven have actually incorporated the commitment from this regional agreement into their national licensing regime (through national policy, regulation and legislation);

  - only four have ever denied arms-export licences on sustainable development grounds: Bulgaria, the Netherlands, Sweden, and the UK;

  - only two – the Netherlands and the UK - have a stated policy of consulting the government department for development in the export decision-making process.

Current commitments under the Wassenaar Arrangement, OSCE and EU

The **Wassenaar Arrangement** is a multilateral forum set up specifically to deal with arms issues. It comprises 33 states, the majority of global arms manufacturers and exporters, including the US, EU member states, a number of Eastern European states, along with Argentina, Canada, Japan, New Zealand, South Korea and Turkey. The **Organisation for Security and Cooperation in Europe (OSCE)** is a wider forum, comprising 55 states in Europe, Central Asia and North America.[109] These two forums have agreed several principles concerning arms transfers and sustainable development

- OSCE Principles Governing Conventional Arms Transfers (1993)

- OSCE Document on Small Arms and Light Weapons (2000)

- Wassenaar Arrangement Best Practice Guidelines for Small Arms and Light Weapons (2002)

which include identical text requiring participating states to take into account:

the nature and cost of the arms to be transferred in relation to the circumstances of the recipient country, including its legitimate security and defence needs and the objective of the least diversion for armaments of human and economic resources.

The **EU Code of Conduct**, agreed in June 1998, aims to set "high common standards which should be regarded as the minimum for the management of, and restraint in conventional arms transfers by all EU Member States." It has a set of eight criteria governing arms transfers. Criterion Eight refers to:

The compatibility of the arms exports with the technical and economic capacity of the recipient country, taking into account the desirability that states should achieve their legitimate needs of security and defence with the least diversion for armaments of human and economic resources.

In considering this Criterion:
Member States will take into account, in the light of information from relevant sources such as UNDP, World Bank, IMF and OECD reports, whether the proposed export would seriously hamper the sustainable development of the recipient country. They will consider in this context the recipient country's relative levels of military and social expenditure, taking into account also any EU or bilateral aid.

Other states surveyed in the research, particularly those in the process of developing regulations on arms exports, have yet to make the link between the two issues and to recognise the importance of incorporating such a provision into arms-licensing policy. **This is clearly unacceptable. Exporting states need to engage more fully with and weigh more carefully the impact of arms transfers on sustainable development, alongside legitimate security needs and against profit, by adopting a thorough and transparent methodology for assessment.**

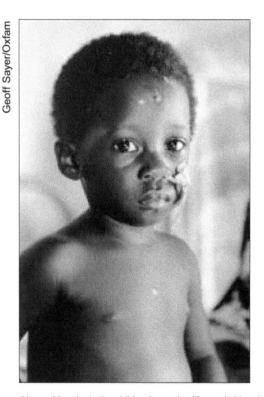

Geoff Sayer/Oxfam

Nancy Musoke in the children's ward at Kagando Hospital, Uganda, where she is being treated for malaria. Like Nancy's mother, many people in developing countries struggle to pay for treatment for themselves or their children. Each year worldwide, 700,000 children under 5 years of age die from malaria and 300 million people contract the illness.
(Statistics from Global Health Council)

Donors recognise the link between governance and the security sector

Increasingly, Western governments are supporting the transformation of the security sectors of developing countries and states in transition, in order to prevent the occurrence of violent conflict.

According to the Guidelines of the **Development Assistance Committee of the Organisation for Economic Cooperation and Development,** 'Security is an essential component of good governance and initiatives to ensure peace and sustainable development. Recognition is growing that what happens in this area has a significant impact on a country's overall prospects for development as well as the effectiveness of international assistance provided in other areas.'

'... the governance approach to security systems recognises that countries have legitimate security needs that must be met efficiently and effectively. It requires a security system with security forces that are the right size, appropriately tasked, and cost effectively equipped. This has implications for the way resources are managed, including the budget planning and execution process.'

'Efforts to improve security expenditure management should be set in the broader context of strengthening the institutional framework in which public spending and security decision-making occurs, ensuring due transparency and attention to corruption.'[110]

Laws and procedures to ensure that security institutions are properly accountable and trained should be based upon international law, particularly international human rights and humanitarian law.

The absence of a strong, standard, or accessible methodology

Approaches to assessing the impact of arms transfers on sustainable development, where they do exist, are generally weak and *ad hoc*. Assessments are therefore neither comprehensive nor consistent.

Clarity and scope

Where governments do discuss sustainable development in the context of arms exports, it is often worded ambiguously. This leaves too much room for interpretation: **arms licensing policy can be construed quite differently across the different national export-control regimes – and even potentially within a national export-control regime**. States can draw different conclusions about the possible negative implications of an arms export for the sustainable development of a recipient country. In borderline cases, the differences in interpretation could be critical.[111]

The UK's assessment methodology

As a result of the interdepartmental discussion led by the Department of Trade and Industry (DTI) after the controversy over the 2001 Watchman export to Tanzania, the UK has developed a three-stage process to identify 'destinations where sustainable development as defined in Criterion Eight [of the EU Code, relating to sustainable development] is likely to be an issue', and to examine in more detail the 'possible impact of the relevant proposed exports on the economy or sustainable development of the recipient country to those destinations'.[112]

1 A list of states is identified that reflects destinations where 'the prevailing macro-economic and development conditions mean that an export is likely to trigger a concern about the economic impact or sustainable development as defined by Criterion Eight.' [113] This list is drawn from the World Bank International Development Association on the basis that it represents the world's poorest countries – currently 81 countries.[114]

2 By referring to this list, the DTI then identifies on a case-by-case basis those export-licence applications it passes on to the Department for International Development (DFID) – the lead department on this criterion – for a closer examination against Criterion Eight, as well as to the Ministry of Foreign Affairs and Ministry of Defence. In addition, DFID is able to ask to view any or all licence applications if it feels they are of concern.

3 For those applications that have been identified as requiring further detailed assessment, the government has designed a series of indicators:

- relative levels of military and social expenditure, and level of military spending as a percentage of GNP;

- aid dependency compared with the regional average;[115]

- the state of public finances;

- balance of payments;

- external debt sustainability;

- economic and social development: GNP per capita and the Human Development Index;

- and the status of any IMF or World Bank-sponsored economic reform programmes.

These indicators aim to take into account both the development situation in the importing country and the potential impacts of the arms transfer. Information about the indicators is pre-compiled by economists and updated annually. DFID's country experts and economists are also involved in the assessment process, to provide detailed opinion and analysis of the situation in the recipient state.

How these indicators are actually measured or used in practice is not disclosed by the UK Government. The UK Government should be more transparent about exactly how countries on the list are assessed, and make available information regarding recommendations by DFID to the Department of Trade and Industry on licences that are actually authorised, so as to allow for more public scrutiny of an assessment.

Both the UK and the Dutch governments use a list of destinations of concern (albeit different lists) as a way of identifying states where the adverse impact on sustainable development from an arms export may be an issue.[116] Both are based on international aid: those qualifying for aid in terms of their relative poverty and lack of creditworthiness in the UK's case, and those receiving aid on the basis of Part One of the OECD DAC List in the case of the Netherlands.

However, **there is a concern that arms exports to states not on the list, where a potential negative impact may occur, could be overlooked in the licensing process**, and as such these proposed exports might inadvertently be granted a licence. Of particular concern are those countries that might not be highly dependent upon aid, or eligible for aid, but where the impact of arms transfers might still have a significant impact on the sustainable development of that country. This is particularly the case for the lower range countries of medium development, where a high value transfer, or the accumulation of such transfers, could have a significant impact on the country's ability to meet its development needs, such as South Africa.

Little is known about how *or* if other governments identify countries of concern through using an initial list.

Identifying exports of concern: value of transfer

Although not specifically related to a concern over sustainable development, the US system of prior notification allows Congress the right to scrutinise some proposed sales if they are above a certain value. Under the Arms Export Control Act, Congress has the right to be notified about transfers with a dollar value above US$14m for major defence equipment, and US$50m for general defence items.[117]

The Senate has tried to raise these thresholds once already, to US$50m and US$100m respectively, and is likely to try to do so again.

Using a monetary threshold alone does have several drawbacks:

- the impact of the cost of a transfer would be very different, depending on the per capita Gross National Income of a recipient state;

- spending by countries below this threshold, but where there could still be an impact upon sustainable development, would be in effect ignored; and

- a single-value threshold would not take into account the cumulative impact a number of transfers might have on the sustainable development of an importing country.

Some states refer to a number of sources when discussing indicators used to make an assessment of the impact of arms transfers on sustainable development. These include reports of the UNDP, International Monetary Fund (IMF), World Bank, and the Organisation for Economic Co-operation and Development (OECD).

While there is a degree of commonality in the indicators used in some cases, there is no discussion of how these indicators relate either to each other or to sustainable development targets and thresholds. Other states do not even identify the reference sources they use. **Since different countries may use different targets and indicators in different combinations or arrangements, approaches are neither consistent nor comparable. More importantly, while states mention the OECD, UNDP, and IMF reports, there is no real evidence of any structure or methodology to form an assessment in the majority of cases. Most states have simply not thought through the assessment process.**

A focus mainly on economic factors

Of the 22 states that responded to the survey, indicators used focus almost entirely on the economic and financial capabilities of the recipient state, as well as on the legitimate defence needs of the country. The latter must be a central part of any assessment process, but it needs to be accompanied by a range of other indicators, economic *and* otherwise, that can capture development, security, and other perspectives in a more holistic way. **Current assessments of the impact of a transfer upon the sustainable development of a country ignore the core concerns that they are supposed to be taking into account.**

The level of military expenditure in comparison with the level of social spending – mainly on health and education – is typically used to assess the effects of military spending on a country's ability to fund 'development'. This provides a useful starting point for assessing potential negative effects. However:

- The economic focus reveals little about other elements of sustainable development, such as human security, social, development, gender equality, and governance.

- Economic indicators only measure the *input* in terms of spending (for example, on education or health) in relation to how much is spent on the military. It does not attempt to consider the *output* of such spending in terms of what is achieved and how efficiently resources are being used.

In the cases of Germany and the United Kingdom, there does appear to be some consideration of indicators other than purely economic ones. Germany makes explicit reference to social justice, social equality, and poverty reduction, while the UK Government's assessment draws on the Human Development Index (HDI). However, as with all approaches, including those that focus on purely economic indicators, there is no consideration of trends over time, so that an assessment of the *direction* a state is taking in spending and development achievements can be made.

In general, for military expenditure to be considered a high economic burden, a threshold is stipulated. The Stockholm International Peace Research Institute (SIPRI) for example, identifies states whose military expenditure represent a high economic burden on the basis that the share of their military expenditure was known to be higher than four per cent of GDP. [118] The Bonn International Centre for Conversion takes into account the cumulative trend (see below[1]).

Figure 3: Low-development countries undergoing a significant process of militarisation according to the BIC3D Index

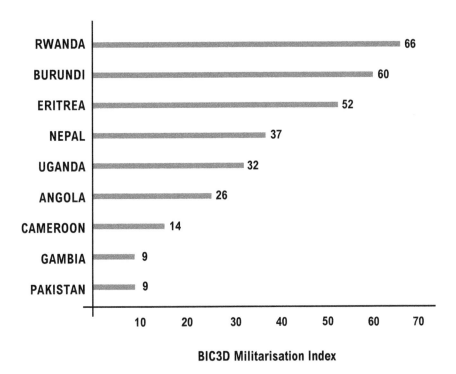

BIC3D Militarisation Index

Source: Bonn International Centre for Conversion, *Conversion Survey 2003*, Nomos Verlagsgesellschaft, Baden-Baden, 2003.

[1] **Assessing levels of militarisation:** The BIC3D is calculated by combining four sets of data: military spending, arms reserves, armed forces personnel, and people employed in arms production. Values in the BIC3D index vary between +100 per cent and -100 per cent, and they are interpreted on the basis of the difference between the current BIC3D figure and the average since the end of the Cold War.
Source: Bonn International Centre for Conversion, *Conversion Survey 2003*, Nomos Verlagsgesellschaft, Baden-Baden, 2003.

However, little information about the thresholds used by governments is made available by exporter states, including whether or not such an internal guideline forms part of their national licensing regimes. This prevents any useful analysis of comparative practice across the different national export-control regimes.

Huambo, in Angola, was destroyed by heavy artillery, yet people still have to live among the ruins.

The Wassenaar Arrangement Recommended Methodology for Assessing the Political/Economic Standing/Status of the State

a. What is the state's military expenditure? What percentage of GDP does it spend on the military? Is the information it gives on its military expenditures open and accurate, or does it seek to conceal the true costs?

b Does the accumulation of conventional weapons by the state exacerbate an already economically insupportable burden of defence? Does it risk economic or social destabilisation, either nationally or regionally?

The methodology was produced to assist Participating States during the deliberation process associated with considering transfers or denials. It is of a non-binding character; decisions on export licensing remain under the national control of each Participating State. Other elements included in the methodology, but not discussed here are: Assessment of Motivation of the State under Study; Regional Balance of Forces and the General Situation in the Region, Operational Capability, and Acquisition of Military Technology.[119]

Lack of transparency

These weaknesses and inconsistencies in the methodology are coupled with a lack of transparency about decision-making processes. This lack of openness dominates the approaches taken by national governments to implementing assessments of the impact of arms transfers on sustainable development.

Parliamentary Scrutiny

Parliaments currently have only a limited role in the scrutiny of arms-export licence applications. Out of the 22 states that responded to the survey, only Sweden and the USA allow for pre-licensing checks by parliament or congress.[120] Otherwise, parliamentary hearings generally only take place after an export has been authorised, and so while they are a useful mechanism for learning lessons and developing policy and practice based on experience, they do not provide the opportunity to influence or change licensing decisions as they occur.

Some government annual reports do include information on the number of licences denied on the grounds of the potential impact on sustainable development. However, for most states, information on denials is either not kept or is not declassified, as is apparently the case in the USA and South Africa, or remains confidential, as is the case in France.

The importance of 'joined-up government'

In order for governments to engage effectively and pragmatically with the impact of arms transfers on sustainable development, different government departments need to work together to decide who is best placed to carry out an assessment, and who can offer advice in the assessment decision-making process. In other words, there needs to be a holistic, co-ordinated, and joined-up approach, drawing on the expertise of a variety of people and government departments. At the very least, all governments should consult their development departments, or equivalent, in the export decision-making process.

4 Context is critical: investigating the relationship between security, governance, arms imports, and sustainable development

Understanding the relationship between governance and arms imports is critical, and should form a central part of an assessment of the potential impact of arms transfers on sustainable development. This should involve moving beyond macro-economic considerations to an investigation of defence procurement and budgeting practices, the stated objectives of the transfer, the extent of involvement of a wider range of actors in the decision-making process, and the degree to which efforts are made to assess any potential impact upon sustainable development. An understanding of these issues could provide the information necessary actually to make the judgement about whether or not to issue an export licence.

Research methodology: case studies

To examine the import side of the arms-transfer process, primary case-study research on arms import decision-making procedures and their impacts on sustainable development was conducted in six countries (Croatia, Ghana, India, Tanzania, Venezuela, and Yemen) during the period November 2003 to February 2004. Secondary research was also undertaken for the cases of Ethiopia, South Africa, and Chile. Project Ploughshares co-ordinated this work and undertook a consolidated analysis.[121]

The research investigated:

- government decision-making and budgeting processes;
- government justifications of arms-import decisions;
- participation and influence of other actors on arms imports and sustainable development decisions;
- and the extent to which there was examination or recognition of the impact of arms imports on sustainable development.

In some cases, it was difficult to disaggregate research about arms transfers from military expenditure in general. The implications of both were recorded in the research and have been used in this report. The conclusions drawn about military expenditure provide useful context information for consideration of a specific arms transfer.

Government decision making

Insights into decision making by governments around the import of arms can be useful in helping to form a detailed picture of the legitimacy of the proposed import. Legitimacy will depend on a number of factors, apart from the potential impact on sustainable development. Nevertheless, research undertaken for this report illustrates that the extent to which there is open debate and discussion about the transfer and its affordability and appropriateness in relation to the development needs of the country should be a key area of concern for exporter governments.

A concentrated and narrow decision-making process

The decision to import arms is normally taken within either a single ministry or by a select group of officials. This may be the Ministry of Defence (as in the cases of Ghana, South Africa, and Croatia), senior armed services staff (as in Venezuela), a body appointed by or close to the presidency (the National Defence Council in Yemen and the Central Command in Ethiopia), or the cabinet (in Tanzania).

Final approval of the budget necessary for arms imports in these cases is narrower still and typically rests with the government Cabinet or President.

> **A snapshot of governance and military spending in South Africa and Chile**
>
> Since 1994, the **South African** government has made a number of far-reaching changes to its arms-procurement decision-making processes, in order to encourage civilian involvement and to ensure that the parliament and the cabinet must approve key projects. In addition, the Government of National Unity has engaged in extensive public debate, through Defence Reviews, on the role of arms exports in foreign policy as well as over major procurement decisions. It has also publicly stated its defence priorities in a White Paper on National Defence.[122]
>
> In comparison, the case of **Chile** illustrates the institutional tendency of a uniquely powerful pressure group within a democratically elected government to exact a large share of the national budget and of imported supplies. According to the Chilean constitution, defence spending cannot fall below 1989 levels in real terms. Introduced by the Pinochet regime, this limitation – the 'Copper Law' – effectively serves to protect the defence budget from economic shocks and political change, including reduced security threats. Moreover, 10 per cent of the revenues from the state-owned copper company, COLDECO, are allocated to the armed forces for arms procurement. Critically, arms purchases from these funds are not subject to congressional approval, thereby preventing citizens, and even their elected representatives, from participating in procurement decision-making.[123]

Degree of involvement of 'development' departments

Of the nine case studies considered, in only one case is there evidence that a department concerned with development needs was included in the import decision-making process. In Ghana, the recent importation of naval vessels was driven by a decision from the National Democratic Congress to revitalise the fishing industry, taken in conjunction with the Ministry of Food and Agriculture, and subcontracted to the Navy.[124]

It is therefore not surprising that **the case-study research illustrates that there are few identifiable and systematic assessments of the development impact of arms procurement by importing governments**. Government decisions to import arms, and their decisions to pursue social and economic development commitments, are generally conducted entirely separately and reflect an ongoing isolation of military programmes from other government responsibilities. Exporter governments are well positioned not only to comment on this relationship, but also potentially to bring military and development thinking closer together.

Budgeting processes and development of economic goals

The case studies reveal the cost of the arms import is included in a defence budget that in turn is a component of the national budget. It is at the level of the national budget that there is the most demonstrable attention to development or to economic goals.

Poverty Reduction Strategy Papers and military expenditure

For the low-development countries under study, Poverty Reduction Strategy Papers (PRSPs) are components of national budgeting. Initiated by the World Bank, the PRSP process encourages more transparent and accountable national budgeting to reduce poverty.

> **The PRSP process**
> At the Annual Meetings of the World Bank Group and the IMF in September 1999, it was agreed that nationally owned participatory poverty-reduction strategies should provide the basis of all World Bank and IMF concessional lending and for debt relief under the enhanced Heavily Indebted Poor Countries (HIPC) Initiative. This approach is reflected in the development of Poverty Reduction Strategy Papers (PRSPs) by country authorities. As of 23 April 2003, 26 full PRSPs had been produced, and 45 Interim PRSPs.[125]

In some instances, the PRSPs also address military spending.

- Ghana's Poverty Reduction Strategy Paper recognises that 'public protection needs to be strengthened', providing a backdrop for the Ghana Armed Forces to present its budget and activities in the context of development.[126]

- In Tanzania, the PRSP was finalised at the same time as the country became a Highly Indebted Poor Country (HIPC) and was negotiating the purchase of the 'Watchman' military air-traffic control system. The PRSP stated that: '… while the budgetary expenditure will continue to be restrained because of macro-economic considerations, special efforts will be made to channel the limited government resources towards the support of key programs and social services under the poverty reduction strategy'. The decision to import the radar system and the debates it touched off in the country signified the first time that the general public had not only debated a defence issue, but also made the link between military spending and social welfare. Before that event, military spending decisions in Tanzania were a state-security matter, excluded from public or even parliamentary discussion.[127]

- Ethiopia's PRSP was finalised in July 2002. In it, the government committed itself to steadily reduce defence expenditure. It was only towards the end of 2003 that the government took the unprecedented step of making public its 'Foreign Affairs and National Security Policy', which stated, 'It is essential that we balance our economic development with our defence requirement.'[128]

- The government of Yemen, in contrast, committed itself to a Poverty Reduction Strategy Paper for 2003–2005 in May 2002, but appeared not to have linked poverty reduction to reduced military expenditures.[129]

A non-PRSP country: Croatia

Even in the absence of the PRSP process, the middle-development country of Croatia effectively directed national expenditure to social needs by reducing military spending as it increased its central budget. The legacy of the armed conflict in former Yugoslavia brought high reconstruction and transition costs that were met in part by reduced military spending after 1997. The rise of government expenditure during this time was due to the high social costs of war and transition, not to military expenditure.[130]

Budgeting practices

While parliaments should play a role in overseeing the national and defence budgets, members of parliament do not necessarily possess the expertise or the political strength to challenge government decisions on military matters. For example, in theory, the military budgeting process in Ghana is subject to Parliamentary debate.[131] In practice, parliamentary discussion is limited by security concerns and lack of expertise, and a recent debate exposed military 'off-budgetary' expenditures not included in the figures presented to Parliament. It is also considered disloyal for parliamentarians to ask too many questions about military budgeting.[132] In Yemen, the executive must present a national budget to the House of Representatives for approval. [133] According to Article 87 of the constitution, parliament 'may not change the proposed budget without the approval of the government.' In practice the concentration of fiscal and political power in the office of the President has led at best to highly centrally controlled arms import activities.[134] In South Africa, the government has amended arms procurement decision-making since 1994 to promote civil society input and to ensure that Parliament approves of key projects, although sceptics maintain that real decisions are made by a few powerful political leaders.[135]

Transparency

The varying degrees of transparency concerning arms-import policy at all levels also profoundly affect the prospects of identifying common standards in budgeting procedures. During the war with Eritrea in 1999–2000, Ethiopia diverted resources from other departments to the Ministry of Defence, presumably in part to pay for substantial war-time weapons imports. These decisions were made *in camera*.[136] The arms-procurement budget process in India, despite an eleven-step set of procedures, is still largely secret. A report in February 2004 sponsored by the government noted that 'the defence procurement system needs some improvement and the deals are secret'.[137] Even in the more open post-apartheid climate of South Africa, the extensive public scrutiny and debate of the large weapons package was preceded by early secrecy, and the government has always opposed publication of the details of the procurement contract.[138] The weapons-import procedures and budgeting of Yemen are allegedly opaque.[139]

Crispin Hughes/Oxfam

Internally displaced children play on an old Russian tank in Eritrea.

Corruption

In many developing countries, corruption has had, and continues to have, devastating consequences for development and stability.[140] There is a broad consensus about the deleterious impact of corruption on economic growth, wealth distribution, and the legitimacy and efficiency of the state.[141] Coupled with arms spending, corruption may fuel unaccountable political decision making that seriously undermines democracy. Corrupt practices in arms transfers are widespread and commonplace. **According to a report by the NGO Transparency International, of all industries ranked in its 1999 'Bribe Payers Index', the arms industry was considered the second most likely to involve bribes.**[142] Despite accounting for less than one per cent of world trade in 1999, estimates from the US Department of Commerce derived from the General Accounting Office (a congressionally funded watchdog agency) show that 50 per cent of all bribes are paid for defence contracts.[143] The report also suggests that a conservative estimate of the value of bribes is 10 per cent of the total value of the trade, or billions of dollars every year.[144] Negotiations for the BAE Hawk purchase by India were halted in 2001, in part because of the resignation of the head of the ruling coalition party Bangaru Laxman over an alleged arms bribery scandal.[145]

The cost of corruption in Croatia

In Croatia during the 1990s, the media discovered many cases of fraud, corruption, abuse, and embezzlement committed by new 'tycoons', protégés of the ruling party, which suggested massive political interference in the economy. Until 1998, many of these cases were connected with Ministry of Defence procurement operations. Croatia's current rating on the Human Development Index (HDI) suggests that the available income has not been used in the best way to induce development. Although Croatia's HDI was 0.809 in 2000, the comparison with some other transition countries shows that Croatia was less successful in channelling income into human development than was, for example, Poland. Public administration and government institutions were apparently incapable of designing policies of economic and social recovery to achieve a level of economic efficiency in Croatia.[146]

Government justifications of arms import decisions

Insight into how governments justify arms imports is useful in assessing the stated and actual need. **The research for this report illustrates that there is a need to look beyond an analysis of military needs *per se* to the political, social, and economic rationale.**
It is therefore important that an assessment methodology is able to ask questions about a range of possible importing government objectives.

The standard expectation of arms-import decisions is that they be made in response to clearly defined military needs and objectives that are lawful in national as well as international law. This is often the case. In Ghana, parliamentary approval of the budget for helicopters was linked to UN operations in the Democratic Republic of Congo. In Croatia, the decision in 2001 to modernise 12 MiG-21 aircraft was meant to retain a minimal air force capability required by the Croatian constitution.[147] The unique Chilean process of military-procurement budgeting involves using dedicated funds generated by the 'Copper Law,' and means that the objectives of the armed services are virtually the sole factors in arms-import decisions.

For India, weapons imports were linked to perceived external security threats and ongoing tensions with Pakistan over the Kashmir region.[148] In Ethiopia, the import of major weapon systems during 1998–2000 has to be viewed in the context of the border conflict with Eritrea.

In situations of violent conflict, exporter governments have to weigh the true costs of arms transfers carefully.

- What level of security response is appropriate, and what else needs to be done to ensure a solution to the conflict?

- Are the benefits of the transfer in meeting legitimate security needs greater than their cost in terms of the impact on the development of the country?

- Even if the legitimate security needs of a state do take precedence, is the importing government likely to abide by international human rights and humanitarian law?

- Are wider processes of reflection about the causes of conflict underway, and is the government committed to addressing them?

Exporter governments must hold importers accountable for the ways in which arms are used, and consider offering packages of support that could include support for military training or reform, peace processes, and follow-up to monitor agreements.

Political objectives

In some cases, however, arms are imported more to meet political objectives than to address security threats. In Croatia, the decision taken in 1999 by the Tudjman government to upgrade its fleet of about 30 MiG-21 fighter aircraft was, at least in part, a political move to improve ties with Israel and, through it, with the West.

Two Croatian MiG-21 and two USAF F-16 fighter aircraft, during a joint Croatian-US exercise over Adriatic Croatian coast, 2002.

Arms deals and isolation in Croatia

Being relatively isolated on the international scene, according to one report, Croatia regarded Israel as an influential intermediary which could facilitate Croatia's rapprochement to international associations such as NATO and the WTO. President Tudjman was apparently hoping that the conclusion of the deal to upgrade 24 MiG-21 fighter aircraft would prompt the Israeli Government to invite him to visit Israel, which would be a major foreign-relations success for the Croatian president. Israel also sensed the opportunity, and the upgrade contract was seemingly the price for extending diplomatic recognition to Croatia.[149] The Israelis could cite their co-operation with Romania, which helped that country to come closer to NATO and other Western alliances and institutions.[150]

In Yemen, evidence cited in a recent study allegedly points to the president's office having used arms imports as a means to maintain and strengthen the kinship and tribal ties upon which it depends politically.[151] The Tanzanian decision to purchase an expensive military air-traffic control system for its air force of 19 aircraft in mixed condition was followed, under internal and external criticism, by 'mission creep', which led to the presentation of the system as one meeting both military and civilian air-traffic needs. This suggests that the purchase of the system could have been intended to meet other objectives, including political ties with the UK, the supplier country.[152]

Social and economic objectives

In the middle-level development nations of Croatia and South Africa, arms-import objectives included industrial benefits intended to bolster employment and the domestic industrial economy.

In South Africa, details of an 'affordability study', revealed as a result of a legal challenge, have suggested that the government did examine the potential social and economic impacts of the large arms deal, and then concluded the deal in spite of the negative findings of the study.[153] The 'offset' package associated with the weapons-procurement programme consisted of promises by a consortium of major companies in France, Germany, Sweden, and the UK to purchase South African goods, to invest in local industry, including the construction of new plants, and to sub-contract parts of the production of the imported military equipment. The promises totalled R70bn, more than twice the value of the imported weapons.[154]

Government interest in economic and other industrial benefits is not confined to middle-development nations. In India, the arms-importing process gives close attention to economic benefits, particularly in recent years, when the government mounted a programme to boost domestic military production.[155] The negotiations for the BAE Hawk contract, for example, included arrangements for most of the aircraft to be assembled in India. Naval vessels were imported in Ghana to protect fishing waters in Ghana, as previously stated, and in Bangladesh.[156]

5 Towards the development of an assessment methodology

Drawing on all of the insights described in this report, it has been possible to develop, in some detail, a draft methodology for ensuring sustainable development is properly assessed in arms-export decision making. It is recognised that this may need to be developed and adapted further but the approach set out below provides a useful starting point for discussion. While the final decision as to whether or not to issue an export licence will always remain a matter of judgement, it is essential that such judgement is rooted in a thorough and transparent assessment methodology. When establishing such an assessment methodology, governments need to be mindful of certain key realities.

- There is a tension between the complexity of the issue and the need to identify a framework sufficiently clear and accessible for exporter governments to use.

- Governments around the world have signed up to Millennium Development Goals.

- Building on the OSCE Principles, criterion 4c of a legally binding Arms Trade Treaty would provide a clear and consistent global basis for assessments, to encourage all governments to take the issue of sustainable development and other relevant export criteria seriously.

- To the maximum extent possible, the assessment methodology should be based on already established and internationally agreed standards concerning development, human rights, arms procurement and legitimate security needs, and publicly available indicators and targets for assessment. It should also draw on development expertise in government and civil society.

The preliminary methodology outlined below therefore serves as a guide for both the implementation of Article 4c of the proposed Arms Trade Treaty, and also for analogous criteria in national, regional, and multilateral export-control arrangements. It is structured around three core elements:

- triggers – to identify transfers of possible concern;

- indicators – to map the development and human security status of these countries;

- factors – to enable deeper context and deal-specific questioning of responsible governance and arms-procurement processes so that an arms-export judgement can be made.

A diagrammatic summary of the methodology is given in Appendix 3, and a summary table in Appendix 4.

No importing country should be singled out unfairly, but by using two sets of trigger questions to begin analysis of the impact of a proposed arms transfer, this approach seeks to be as thorough as possible in alerting cases of concern. The triggers can help to identify transfers of concern that require further consideration, but without pre-supposing which countries may be involved.

The methodology requires the level of development of the country to be ascertained first, and then to consider whether the value of the transfer is significant enough to trigger concerns over the impact on sustainable development.

Trigger 1: What is the level of development?

- **Measure:** Human Development Index (HDI) Value

The Human Development Index is a summary measurement of human development. It measures the average achievements in a country in three basic dimensions of human development:

- - long and healthy lives, as measured by life expectancy at birth;
- - knowledge, as measured by the adult literacy rate (with two-thirds weight) and the combined primary, secondary, and tertiary gross education enrolment ratio (with one-third weight);
- - a decent standard of living, as measured by GDP per capita (PPP US$).

The HDI value therefore gives a snapshot picture of a country's relative development situation. The filtering process should consider a country's HDI value over a ten-year period in order to gain an idea of how the development situation of the country may or may not be changing (Human Development Index Trends). Both a steady decrease and any negative anomalies should be taken into account.

Threshold: For countries with an HDI of less than 0.65 – proceed to Trigger 2a.

Threshold: For countries with an HDI of between 0.65 and 0.85 – proceed to Trigger 2b.

For other countries – no further analysis on sustainable development grounds is required.

Trigger 2a: For countries of low development, is this a financially-significant transfer?

- **Measure:** Value of transfer as a percentage of GDP

Threshold: Value of transfer as a percentage of GDP = 0.002% or more

This measurement can provide an indication of how much the national budget would need to be increased in order to take into account the value of the transfer, and by implication the possible impact on how a government would cope with any increased demands and allocation of resources to development.

This threshold has been set purposefully low in order to filter out only the smallest, financially least significant transfers. In order to make this methodology workable, it is neither necessary nor pragmatic to undertake a full analysis for every single transfer, no matter how small, hence this trigger will only select significant transfers for analysis.

If this threshold is reached – i.e. if the transfer value is greater than 0.002% of GDP – then full analysis is required.

If the transfer was not found to be financially significant, but it is part of a bigger arms deal which may be, analysis should move to trigger 2c.

Trigger 2b: Is this transfer of such a scale that it might have an impact even on countries with relatively high development?

- **Measure:** Value of transfer as a percentage of GDP

Threshold:[157] Value of transfer as a percentage of GDP = 0.0275% or more

Again, this analysis is required to judge whether the size of the transfer in relation to GDP should be considered.

However in this case, the threshold is much higher. It is attempting to identify those transfers above a certain financial value which could still have an impact on the country's level of development.

If this threshold is reached – i.e. if the transfer value is greater than 0.0275% of GDP – then full analysis is required.

If this is not triggered - if the transfer was not found to be financially significant - but it is part of a bigger arms deal which may be, analysis should move to trigger 2c.

Trigger 2c: Is this transfer one element of a bigger deal?

- If so, measure the financial value of the total deal or contract as a percentage of GDP

Threshold: Same as threshold used for trigger 2a or 2b, depending on level of development

Including this consideration is vital because large arms deals are often broken down into smaller elements – South Africa is a case in point. The US$6bn deal consisted of several elements from several different suppliers. This trigger should also be able to take into account the transfer of components.

If this threshold is reached, a full analysis is required. If the threshold is not reached, there is no need for further analysis on sustainable development grounds.

Table 2: Simulation of the proposed trigger methodology

Data concerning the arms transfer

Importer	Exporter	Transfer	Year	Transfer value US$m	GDP USbn
Ethiopia	Russia	2 Mi-24V/Mi-35 Hind-E combat helicopters, Su-27 fighter aircraft and Mi-8 helicopters	1999	155	6.5
Tanzania	UK	'Watchman' radar system	2001	40	9.3
Yemen	Poland	3 Deba Class landing craft and 1 Polnocny Class landing ship	2002	50	10.4
Ghana	USA	Upkeep of 2 naval dept vessels @ $1m per year each over ten years	1999–2000	20	7.7
Ghana	USA	4 MH7 Helicopters, 2 for peacekeeping	2002	19.5	6.0
India	Russia	Admiral Gorshkov aircraft carrier	2004	1,500	515.0
South Africa	Germany, UK, France, Sweden	The deal included: frigates, submarines, aircraft, and helicopters	1999	6,000	131.0
Venezuela	Brazil	8 AMX-T fighter/trainer aircraft	2001	150	126.0
Venzuela	Italy	12 SF-260M trainer aircraft	2000–2001	12	126.0
Croatia	Israel	Upgrade of 24 MiG-21s	1999	120	19.9
Chile	US	10 F-16 Fighter Jets	2002	636	64.2
Croatia	Romania	Upgrade of 12 MiG-21s	2000–2001	8.5	19.5

Notes
Values of GDP and HDI were taken from the closest available year to that of the transfer

Trigger 1	Trigger 2a		Trigger 2b	
HDI	Transfer value as a % of GDP >0.002% to trigger	Analysis required?	Transfer value as a % of GDP >0.0275% to trigger	Analysis required?
0.321	2.40%	Yes		
0.400	0.43%	Yes		
0.470	0.48%	Yes		
0.542	0.26%	Yes		
0.567	0.32%	Yes		
0.590	0.29%	Yes		
0.702			4.58%	Yes
0.775			0.12%	Yes
0.775			0.01%	No
0.803			0.60%	Yes
0.813			0.99%	Yes
0.818			0.04%	Yes

Sustainable development and small arms and light weapons (SALW)

The Arms Trade Treaty, proposed by Oxfam, Amnesty International, the Arias Foundation, Project Ploughshares, Saferworld, the Federation of American Scientists and other NGOs in the International Action Network on Small Arms and most multilateral approaches to date primarily take into account the **misuse** of small arms in separate criteria from those concerned with sustainable development. Following the methodology suggested here, most sales of SALW would not raise concerns via trigger 2 relating to the value of the transfer, although some more expensive sales may. However, their impact – in terms of the consequences of their misuse for sustainable development – is likely to be felt most keenly in countries with low HDI values. The transfers of concern are therefore likely to have been flagged up using the HDI filter and the actual consequences of how SALW could impact upon sustainable development, and the likelihood of the weapons being misused can then be assessed at the levels of indicators and factors. Therefore, while being of primary concern in other criteria, there is still room for a specific consideration of the impact of SALW on sustainable development.

Indicators: information gathering

Having identified that a potential export to a country raises concerns, the next stage in the assessment process is to gather information about the sustainable development situation of that country. The indicators used by governments and official agencies in approaches to date have an economic focus. This is certainly a useful starting point for analysis: the most obvious and immediate implications of arms spending are macro-economic in character. But it is also possible to achieve a deeper understanding of the sustainable development context of the country in question by using internationally recognised indicators that provide a fuller picture of the areas of development that the transfer could affect. The following range of indicators should be referred to in order to build up the fullest picture of a country's development situation. They cover four key areas of concern:

- **economic context,** in order to assess the economic impact of the arms transfer;

- **the Millennium Development Goals,** in order to assess the possible impact of the proposed import on progress in achieving the MDGS;

- **gender in development,** in order to gauge the possible impact of the diversion of social spending or the misuse of arms against women;

- **security,** in order to assess the general security situation of the country.

The process of assessment by these indicators should be governed by two key principles.

-   A consideration of **actual figures and trends**: both are needed, to identify absolute value and also to identify whether the country's performance is actually improving or declining. Bangladesh and Congo Brazzaville are cases in point: both received an HDI score of 0.502 in 2001. However, in 1985, Bangladesh had scored 0.384 and has experienced a steady improvement since. By contrast, Congo Brazzaville scored 0.553 in 1985, witnessing a steady decrease since then.

- A consideration of both **inputs and outputs**. It is not sufficient just to consider how much is spent by a country on for example, health and education. An assessment should also be made of the achievements of this spending in terms of improvements, efficiency, and performance. What has the actual impact of the spending been on securing internationally recognised economic and social rights? A country spending a lot of money on health and education may not necessarily be investing in a manner that will support sustainable development. For example, India spends more on education that on the military, but it still has the highest rate of illiteracy in the world.

Input

1 The economic context

The following questions should be answered by considering the indicators below over a ten-year period, either taking an average over the period, or using judgement about the trends.

1a. Does the government illustrate balanced spending priorities?

An assessment of how much a government allocates to different sectors of its budget and its major projects illustrates the relative priorities of government spending.

Measurements:

- Military expenditure as a percentage of GDP

- Military expenditure as a percentage of (Education and Health) expenditure

1b. What is the country's level of aid dependency?

An understanding of a country's aid dependency can be a powerful indicator when seen in relation to the cost of an import.

Measurements:

- Official development assistance received, as a percentage of GDP

- Net foreign direct investment flows, as a percentage of GDP

- Total debt service as a percentage of GDP

- Where applicable, the Highly Indebted Poor Country decision point – whereby the World Bank sets out the eligibility of a country for debt relief and sets the level of debt relief

1c. What is the overall trading situation of the country?

Information about a country's balance of trade provides a means of assessing the impact of the value of the transfer on the overall trading situation of the importing country.

Measurement:

* The balance of trade in goods and services

1d. What would the impact of the import be on the country's economic growth?

The datasets below provide the statistics necessary to consider the significance of the potential impact of an import on a country's economic growth.

Measurements:

* GDP per capita
* GDP per capita annual growth rate as a percentage
* Fiscal deficit

Output

2 The Millennium Development Goals

2a. What is the situation of the country vis-à-vis the Millennium Development Goals?

2b. How could the arms transfer affect the country's progress in achieving the MDGs?

Annie Bungeroth/Oxfam

To make a meagre profit, these two long-term refugee boys from Afghanistan, Allahwadin and Zahreen, sort rubbish in the Quetta region of Pakistan. They earn 2 rupees (US$ 0.045) per kilo of paper, and 30 rupees (about 70 US cents) for plastic bottles.

The Millennium Development Goals represent a valuable addition to the datasets described above, because they measure progress over time in relation to internationally agreed development targets (see chapter 1). They therefore give an indication of the overall development situation of the country in relation to these targets – a valuable measurement when considering the possible impact of an arms transfer on sustainable development.

By 2015, the Millennium Development Goals aim to:

1   Halve extreme poverty and hunger
2   Achieve universal primary education
3   Promote gender equality and empower women
4   Reduce child mortality
5   Improve maternal health
6   Combat HIV/AIDS, malaria, and other diseases
7   Ensure environmental sustainability
8   Develop a global partnership for development

The UNDP Human Development Reports measure combined progress in achieving the specific targets outlined in the MDGs on a country-by-country basis. The assessment of countries' achievements is based on the following criteria:

- *Achieved*: the country has already achieved the target.
- *On track:* the country has attained the rate of progress needed to achieve the target by 2015 or has attained 90 per cent of that rate of progress.
- *Lagging:* the country has achieved 70–89 per cent of the rate of progress required to archive the target by 2015.
- *Far behind:* the country has achieved less than 70 per cent of the required rate of progress.
- *Slipping back:* the country's level of achievement is at least 5 percentage points worse over a 10-year assessment period.

The MDG Country Reports

Each country also produces its own MDG report, and these are expected to be completed by the end of 2004, potentially providing another level of detail for exporter governments to turn to in making an assessment. The information and analysis for the Country Reports is provided by the United Nations Country Teams in close collaboration with the government, based on available official statistics. These reports have several purposes:

- to provide a convenient update on the progress of individual countries in meeting their individual development targets and reducing poverty;
- to describe the development challenges which confront each country in meeting the targets;
- to outline the nature of the supporting policy environment;
- to identify the specific areas in which development co-operation can assist;
- to highlight the needs for strengthening data-gathering and statistical capacity-building.

3   Gender in development

Despite the evidence of the impact of arms transfers on gender inequalities in terms of social spending and the misuse of arms, no assessment takes this into account to date. The MDG gender measurement considers the ratio of boys to girls in primary, secondary, and tertiary education; the ratio of literate females to males; the female share of non-agricultural wage employment; and the percentage of seats in parliament held by women. In addition, the following question and *measurements*, covering a ten-year period, should be considered:

What is the status and level of respect accorded to women's rights?

Measurements:

- The number of rural women living in conditions of economic underdevelopment and social marginalisation
- The level of access to healthcare and related services
- The prevalence of violence against women, including armed violence against women

4   Security

Current assessment approaches say very little about security, even though there are readily available datasets that can be drawn on to build up a picture of the level of vulnerability in a country.

How secure do people feel inside the country?

Systematic internal repression, indiscriminate attacks on civilians during armed conflict and the forced movement of people inside and outside of a country can serve as a stark indication of insecurity. In addition, high levels of violent crime and unlawful killings can indicate a highly insecure environment.

Measurements:

- The number of internally displaced people
- The number of refugees by country of asylum and country of origin
- The rate of violent crime and existence of a pattern of unlawful killings/injuries

Assessment should consider a ten-year period.

The information derived from an assessment of these four groups of indicators provides the basis to begin asking detailed questions that are specific to arms and arms transfers.

Factors: arriving at a judgement

The third and final level of assessment considers the critical factors around which the decision of whether or not to grant an export licence will be made. These should focus on governance, the arms-procurement process, the import rationale, and importer capacity. It is at this level of analysis that trade-offs and the weighing up of costs will occur.

The insights from these questions should be viewed in conjunction with the information gathered by the indicators described above. While the information required to answer these questions may not always be easily obtainable, the assessment process should make all efforts to collect as much information at this level of analysis as is possible.

1 Responsible Governance

Factors around governance are crucial in order to assess the level of responsibility of the government financially and in terms of the way the imported arms may be used.

There is a clear relationship between governance standards and military spending.[158] At a meeting in 1997[159], donors formally recognised that the defence-spending decision-making process pursued by a government influences its spending priorities. Research, as well as government statements, suggest that transparent, accountable, and participatory processes for defence-spending decision making are more likely to produce 'appropriate' spending policies that take into account development needs.[160] Such processes are also likely to apply to appropriate spending on law enforcement.

Security Sector Standards

An informed, lawful, and transparent governance system is more likely to identify the legitimate security needs of a country if it is based upon objectives consistent with international law, especially international human rights and humanitarian law. **Where defence-spending decision making is not transparent, accountable, and participatory, and based upon legitimate security needs and international standards, the impact of arms transfers can have significant negative effects upon the country's sustainable development.**

* Is there an informed, lawful, and transparent governance system in control of the security sector institutions?

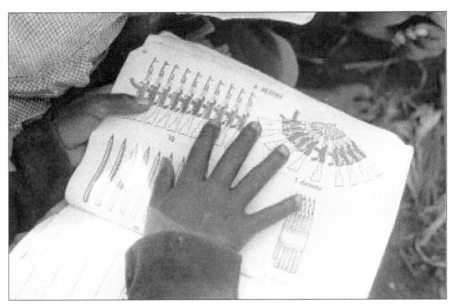

Jenny Matthews/Oxfam

Guns are a major part of life in Angola – they have even been used to teach children how to count.

One possible measurement for governance standards is the World Bank's **aggregated governance indicator** that calculates the median value of six components relating to governance.

- The presentation of accounts
- Political stability and the absence of violence
- Governmental effectiveness
- Procedural guarantees
- The rule of law
- The control of corruption[161]

Another set of standards to assess governance, which is rooted in existing international law and legally binding treaties, is the collection of treaties, principles, rules, guidelines and customary international laws that constitute **international civil and political rights standards.**

- Does the government observe civil and political rights as enshrined in the International Covenant on Civil and Political Rights?

This Covenant has been ratified by most states and stands as an important legal benchmark for governance standards.

During armed conflict, another set of legally binding standards also needs to be promoted and observed by governments – these are embodied in **international humanitarian law.**

To be credible, the assessment should take into account any credible evidence of the violation of these standards within a ten-year period.

- Are the violations persistent, or even widespread and systematic? Does the government condone the violations? Are those responsible for the violations given impunity?

Responsible use of weapons

- Does the government's past history demonstrate that it uses its weapons

  - for lawfully stated needs;
  - responsibly – according to international human rights and humanitarian law;
  - without allowing them to be diverted?

- Are the security personnel suitably qualified and trained to operate and manage the imported equipment lawfully?

- Is there evidence of destruction of economic and social infra- structure by the use of weapons that was not proportionate to military objectives?

The right to sell and purchase weapons confers responsibilities and legal obligations. States do not have the right to use unlimited force, and weapons must be used such that they do not violate international human rights standards or international humanitarian law.

Insights into government budgeting and the decision making behind the import of arms can offer a useful way to start forming a detailed picture of the legitimacy of the proposed import. The following questions should be asked:

Transparency and accountability

- How transparent are state military expenditures and procurement?[162] That is, to what degree is arms procurement decision making in the importing country an open process?

- Is there parliamentary oversight of the military procurement process, and are the parliamentarians adequately informed (for example, is there a committee or hearing process, or are defence reviews conducted, and are these open to public debate)?

- Are the armed forces and law enforcement agencies of the potential recipient sufficiently trained and accountable in terms of international humanitarian law (e.g. the Geneva Conventions) and international human rights standards (e.g. the UN Basic Principles on the Use of Force by Law Enforcement Officials)?

Corruption

- Is there evidence of or suspicion of past corruption in government procurement practices?

Clarity

- Is there a clear and consistent approach to military and law enforcement budgeting?[163] In particular, does there exist a well-defined defence and law enforcement policy and a clear articulation of a country's legitimate security needs that is consistent with international law?

Development commitment

- Has the state made development commitments such as poverty-reduction targets consistent with its international obligations?

- How successful has the government been in meeting these targets, or even attempting to address the country's most critical development needs?

Participation

The extent of knowledge and commentary of sources beyond government officials is a useful indication of the degree of transparency of decision making, and should be incorporated into an assessment methodology. It also provides a glimpse into how other actors view the arms-import process. **The research suggests that bodies and actors external to the ruling government may affect the formulation of national budgets, yet typically they have limited influence on arms budgeting or importing decisions.** The following questions should be asked:

- Does there exist a national defence and law enforcement community to discuss, analyse, and make proposals regarding defence priorities in general, and arms acquisitions in particular?

- Is arms-procurement information available to civil society groups, and are these groups able to participate meaningfully in arms-procurement decision making?

- Does the arms budgeting process allow for input from government departments responsible for development targets (for example, the Ministry of Agriculture)?

3   Rationale: appropriateness and affordability

As discussed in chapter 4, an insight into how governments justify arms imports is useful in assessing the stated and actual need and the suitability of the import in relation to that need. The following questions should be asked:

How appropriate is the import?

- Does the imported equipment directly address security requirements consistent with development targets?

- If not, how is the import justified in terms of security, political, or other needs, and are these justifications legitimate?

  Unless legitimate security needs form a central issue in making an arms-export judgement, the methodology will be flawed. The following line of questioning around *legitimate security needs* has been developed by Malcolm Chalmers of the University of Bradford, bearing in mind Articles 51, 55 and 26 of the UN Charter:

  - If the import is justified in terms of security and political needs, is the strategy on the whole being pursued in a manner that is compatible with minimum global standards – for example in terms of compliance with UN resolutions, respect for international human rights standards, etc.?
  - Even if this is so, is this the 'right' security strategy from a military and political point of view, given the government's overall strategic objectives? Or at least, is there a respectable case for it?
  - Is the trade-off between security and other objectives the 'right' one?

  Answering these questions will always be a matter of judgement. However, the critical point is that the most useful indicators and lines of questioning have been followed, so that the legitimate security needs of a country can be weighed alongside an assessment of its development situation in a manner consistent with international standards. This way the decision that is taken can be made transparently and be justified according to established principles of international law. [164]

- In any case, is the import appropriate to the needs identified?

How affordable is the import?

- Has the importing state conducted an extensive and comprehensive cost–benefit analysis of specific arms deals?

- Has the importing state conducted an 'affordability study' or equivalent, that assesses the impact of arms imports on other government programmes both in terms of immediate costs and also of medium- and long-term costs?[165]

In any case, the exporter also needs to conduct an assessment of the financial capability of the recipient state, by asking the following questions:

- Does the import represent an additional burden to the agreed military or law enforcement spending sector of the budget? If so, at the expense of which other sectors?

- Is the cost of the import fair, in terms of the equipment that it comprises and the stated needs of the importing state?

- Will the import affect the medium- and long-term development goals of the PRSP, and/or of the MDGs for the country concerned?

What is the cumulative impact?

- How does this impact change when the cumulative context is taken into account?

It is often difficult to elucidate the direct impacts of a *particular* weapons import on the sustainable development of the recipient country. Including cumulative assessment in the overall methodology could be critical for a full understanding of the impact on sustainable development of the individual transfer in question, as the significance of the transfer in more general military expenditure trends can be appreciated. One indicator of excessive cumulative spending might be an increase of 10% or more in the percentage change in annual arms procurement, calculated over a five year average.[166]

4 Importer capacity

An assessment of the industrial, technological, and military/law enforcement technical capacity of the country is important for two reasons. First, it is in the first two areas where potential positive impacts are often argued in terms of offsets, industrialisation, and transfer of technology. Secondly, if the military/law enforcement technical capacity of the importer state is not sufficient to responsibly use and maintain the imported equipment, the arms purchase will be wasted or abused.

Industrial and technological capacity

- What is the level of industrialisation of the country in question?

- How would the proposed import build upon the country's technological capabilities? For example:

  - Is there sufficient human capital to make any transfer of technology self-sustaining?

- Does the country have access to the necessary material resources to maintain and further advance technology?
- Would achieving such access be costly?

- What would be the immediate and long-term impacts on the country's job markets and industrial growth?

Technical capacity

- Does professional law enforcement capacity exist at all levels to ensure the transfer is not diverted to illegitimate end users?

- Does the appropriate infrastructure exist to make use of the imported equipment, for example, in terms of runways, roads, or otherwise?

- Are there personnel with the right skills and management system to maintain the imported equipment?

A holistic strategy

The adoption of this methodology by exporter governments would address many of the critical weaknesses and insights that the different stages of research discussed in this report have elucidated. However, in order for assessments of the impact of arms transfers on sustainable development to be most effective, a holistic strategy needs to be adopted. **Alongside, and in conjunction with the methodology recommended here, exporter governments must:**

- **establish a clear mandate and responsibility for their development agencies based upon international law and standards relating to the use of force and to sustainable development,** as well as ensuring that all relevant government departments co-ordinate and co-operate in export-licensing decision making;

- **implement this methodology based upon internationally recognised standards applied consistently and transparently,** so that all exports of concern are accorded equal importance according to objective procedures, and the reasons and evidence for making a judgement can be open to public scrutiny;

- **undertake thorough assessments of the full costs to importers prior to agreement,** including the costs of maintenance and overhaul; training of staff in use; infrastructure; and long-term management costs. The exporter should help the importer to do this; and

- **support the establishment of the proposed International Arms Trade Treaty,** so that the obligation of taking the impact of arms transfers on sustainable development into account is universal and binding in its application, and licences refused by one exporter are not granted by another.

There is also a critical role to be played by international and non-government development organisations. Strong foundations exist in many states – in terms of human rights legislation and export-control legislation – that development organisations can build upon to advocate for a more thorough approach to assessing the critical relationship of arms transfers and sustainable development. To make this happen these organisations need to:

- **talk to exporter governments to explain and elucidate the importance of the arms transfer–sustainable development relationship**, reminding them of their current commitments under multilateral and regional legislation and international human rights standards;

- **urge exporter governments to do all that they can to improve their assessment practices** in line with the recommendations of this report, and offer support and expertise in this process;

- **work together to establish the proposed international Arms Trade Treaty** and advocate for the global implementation of the standards it proclaims.

Appendices

Appendix 1: Selected foundations for sustainable development

- Articles 1(3), 55 and 56 of the 1945 UN Charter are binding on member states and require them to promote and encourage respect and observance of human rights to achieve, amongst other things, 'higher standards of living, full employment and conditions of economic and social progress and development.'

- In 1976, the most basic treaty on economic rights setting out 'freedom from fear and want' – the International Covenant on Economic, Social and Cultural Rights - entered into force and has been ratified by a majority of states, requiring them to contribute to the progressive realisation of these rights through international assistance and co-operation.

- In 1992, at the UN sponsored Earth Summit in Rio de Janeiro attended by 152 world leaders, sustainable development was enshrined in 'Agenda 21'. The Agenda stated that, 'Human beings are at the centre of concerns for sustainable development,' and 'are entitled to a healthy and productive life in harmony with nature'. The agenda pointed to the 'essential task of eradicating poverty as an indispensable requirement for sustainable development'.[167]

- The Declaration of the 1993 UN World Conference on Human Rights stated that, 'the right to development is an inalienable human right and an integral part of fundamental human freedoms'.[168]

- In 1994, the United Nations Development Programme (UNDP) Human Development Report made explicit the connection between the concept of sustainable development and a new concept of *human security*. Human security was defined as: 'safety from such chronic threats as hunger, disease and repression' and 'protection from sudden and hurtful disruptions in the patterns of daily life – whether in homes, in jobs or in communities'.[169] The report also identified the areas of security with which human security was concerned: economic, food, health, environmental, personal, community, and political security. **Human security can therefore be viewed as a description of the condition that sustainable development seeks to achieve, and in considering the potential impact of arms transfers on sustainable development, it is these areas that are of central concern.** [170]

- At the UN Fourth Global Conference on Women in 1995, these connections, and their particular significance for women, were clearly pronounced. The Platform for Action proclaimed: 'Absolute poverty and the feminization of poverty, unemployment, the increasing fragility of the environment, continued violence against women and the widespread exclusion of half of humanity from institutions of power and governance underscore the need to continue the search for development, peace and security and for ways of assuring people-centred sustainable development'.[171]

Regional commitments to improve sustainable development have also been made by groups of developing countries, for example the:

- Intergovernmental Authority on Development (IGAD), established in 1996, aims to 'expand the areas of regional co-operation, increase the members' dependency on one another and promote policies of peace and stability in the region in order to attain food security, sustainable environmental management and sustainable development'.[172]

- New Partnership for Africa's Development (NEPAD), established in 2001, 'is based on a common vision and a firm and shared conviction that its members have a pressing duty to eradicate poverty and to place their countries, both individually and collectively, on a path of sustainable growth and development, and at the same time to participate actively in the world economy and body politic'.[173]

Appendix 2: Summary of principles of the proposed Arms Trade Treaty

The proposed Arms Trade Treaty (ATT - also known as the Framework Convention on International Arms Transfers) focuses on commitments of States in respect of the international transfer of arms. It proceeds on the basis that important related issues such as brokering, licensed production, and end-use monitoring will be addressed in subsequent protocols.

The basic principle of the ATT, set out in **Article 1,** is that all international arms transfers shall be authorised by the appropriate government authority in accordance with its national law. The national law should contain the minimum requirements to be set out in an annex to the ATT, such as that each application for an authorisation should be reviewed and licensed individually. The ATT Principles are to be applied as a minimum and shall not prejudice the application of any more stringent national, regional, or international rules, instruments, or requirements.

Articles 2, 3, and 4 of the ATT contain the main obligations of governments when authorising arms transfers.

Article 2 codifies existing limitations under international law on States' freedom to transfer and to authorise transfers of arms. These limitations include:

* those prohibitions that arise out of the **Charter of the United Nations** (including decisions of the Security Council, such as arms embargoes);

* any **international treaty** to which a State is already bound, including embargoes adopted by other international and regional bodies established pursuant to a treaty (such as the EU), as well as other agreements containing prohibitions of arms, such as the 1997 Anti-personnel Mines Convention;

* universally accepted principles of **international humanitarian law** including the prohibition on the use of arms that are incapable of distinguishing between combatants and civilians or are of a nature to cause superfluous injury or unnecessary suffering. The prohibition on transfers follows from the appreciation that the transfer of such arms would be irreconcilable with the per se prohibition under international humanitarian law of the use of such arms. This prohibition would also cover arms the use of which is prohibited by a specific convention but where the convention does not address the question of transfers;

* those arising under or pursuant to **customary international law**. In some circumstances, arms transfers from one State to another or to persons in the territory of another State without the latter State's consent will amount to a breach of existing obligations under customary international law relating, for example, to the threat or use of force. Transfers to persons other than those exercising governmental authority may also amount to a breach of the principle of non-intervention in the internal affairs of the State.

Article 3 contains limitations based on the use or likely use of the weapon. This article encompasses the widely accepted principle of international law that a State will not participate in the internationally wrongful acts of another State, as stated in Article 16 of the UN International Law Commission's *Articles on Responsibility of States for Internationally Wrongful Acts*. Therefore, governments have a responsibility to ensure that the weapons they transfer are not used illegally. The transfer must not proceed if a State knows or ought to know that the arms will be:

- used for breaches of the UN Charter, in particular the prohibition on the threat or use of force in Article 2(4) and related principles concerning threats to the peace, breaches of the peace, and acts of aggression in Article 39 of the Charter, in General Assembly *Declaration of Principles of International Law* of 1970 (General Assembly Resolution 2625 (XXV) of 1970) and in other standard-setting United Nations resolutions;

- used for serious violations of human rights, including violations of the non-derogable provisions of key international conventions such as the 1966 International Covenant on Civil and Political Rights, the 1950 European Convention for the Protection of Fundamental Rights and Freedoms, the 1969 American Convention on Human Rights and the 1980 African Charter on Human and Peoples' Rights, and widely accepted multilateral conventions such as the 1984 Convention against Torture and Other Cruel, Inhuman and Degrading Treatment or Punishment;

- used for serious violations of international humanitarian law, including grave breaches of the 1949 Geneva Conventions as well as violations of fundamental principles of international humanitarian law contained in other standard-setting multilateral agreements and in customary international law;

- used in the commission of genocide or crimes against humanity; or

- diverted and used to commit any of the above.

Article 4 does not contain prohibitions on the authorisation of arms transfers. Rather, it contains three other factors that governments are required to consider before authorising an arms transfer. These factors take into account the possible effect of the transfer of arms. Specifically, governments are to consider whether the arms are likely to:

- be used for or to facilitate the commission of violent crimes;

- adversely affect regional security and stability;

- adversely affect sustainable development; or

- be diverted and used to commit any of the above.

Where such circumstances are apparent, the Article establishes a presumption against authorisation.

Article 5 of the ATT would require States to establish authorisation and licensing mechanisms under their national laws to effectively implement the convention. The legal system of each State would therefore act as the primary enforcement mechanism for the treaty. An Annex (still to be drafted) will develop minimum standards addressing such matters as the need for a transaction-by-transaction licensing mechanism, minimum disclosure requirements by applicants for licences, mechanisms for parliamentary scrutiny, etc.

Article 6 of the ATT would create an International Registry of International Arms Transfers to which contracting parties would be required to submit an annual report on international arms transfers. Although the United Nations has already established a similar Conventional Weapons Register, it does not include all types of weapons, such as small arms, and is not tied to the implementation of a set of normative standards.

Appendix 3: Graphic presentation of proposed methodology for assessing the impact of arms transfers on sustainable development

The methodology for assessing the impact of arms transfers on sustainable development: Is analysis required?

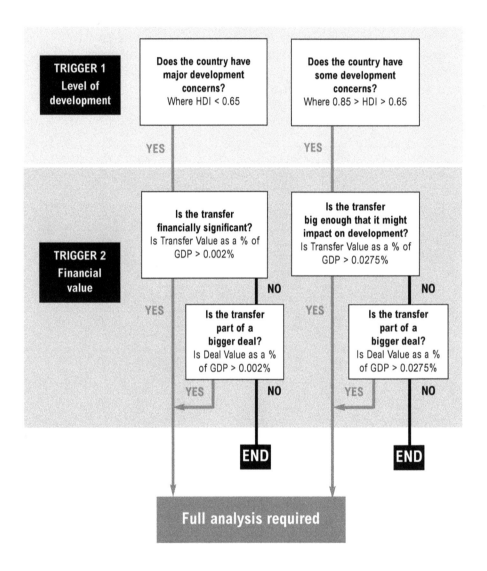

The methodology for assessing the impact of arms transfers on sustainable development: What analysis is required?

	Economic	MDGs	Gender	Human Security
INDICATORS Gathering information	• Public spending priorities • Flows of aid, private capital, and debt • Structure of trade • Economic trends	• Poverty and hunger • Maternal health • Primary education • HIV/AIDS, malaria, and other diseases • Gender equality • Environmental sustainability • Child mortality • Global partnership for development	• Inclusion, and the provision of services • The prevalence of violence against women, including armed violence against women	• Number of IDPs • Number of refugees • The rate of violent crime and existence of a pattern of unlawful killings/injuries

FACTORS
Making a judgement

RESPONSIBLE GOVERNANCE

To form a picture of the type of governance system – issues of:

Security sector standards – Is there an informed, lawful, and transparent governance system in control of the security sector institutions and does the government observe civil and political rights and uphold the standards set in international humanitarian law?

Responsible use of weapons – does history suggest that the imported weapons will be used for lawfully stated needs; responsibly by security personnel suitably qualified and trained to operate and manage imported equipment – according to international human rights and humanitarian law, and without widespread social and economic destruction?

PROCUREMENT

To start forming a detailed picture of the legitimacy of the decision to import – issues of:

Transparency and accountability – how open and transparent is military expenditure and arms procurement and how accountable are the armed forces and law enforcement agencies in terms of international humanitarian law and international human rights standards?

Corruption – is corruption an issue?

Clarity – is there a clear approach to military and law enforcement budgeting, defence and law enforcement policy, and the country's legitimate security needs?

Development commitment – is the state addressing development needs through PRSPs or other mechanisms consistent with its international obligations?

Participation – is there wider involvement, including civil society and government departments responsible for development?

RATIONALE

To assess the suitability of the import against the stated and actual need – issues of:

Appropriateness – how is the import justified – security, political, or other needs – and are these justifications legitimate?

Affordability – will the import affect other government programmes, in particular development goals (PRSPs, MDGs)? Does the import represent value for money?

Cumulative impact – does this import represent a worrying increase in military or law enforcement expenditure?

CAPACITY

To assess whether the importer can benefit from the import – issues of:

Industrial and technological capacity – can the importer really reap potential positive benefits - offsets, industrialisation, and technology transfer?

Technical capacity – does the importer have the skills/infrastructure to manage, use, operate, and maintain the imported equipment?

Appendix 4: Summary of proposed methodology for assessing the impact of arms transfers on sustainable development

Triggers: identifying transfers of concern	Measurements
1 What is the level of development?	For HDI less than 0.65, proceed to 2a For HDI between 0.65 and 0.85, proceed to 2b
2a For low-development countries, is this a financially significant transfer?	Value of transfer as a % of GDP **Threshold:** 0.002% or more
2b Is this transfer of such a scale that it might impact even on countries with relatively high development?	Value of transfer as a % of GDP **Threshold:** 0.0275% or more
2c Is this transfer one element of a bigger deal?	Financial value of the total deal, or contract % of GDP **Thresholds**: as above

Indicators: information gathering	Measurements
Input	
1 *The economic context:* to assess the economic impact of the arms transfer;	
1a Priorities in public spending	Milex as a % of GDP and Milex as a % of (education and health) expenditure
1b Flows of aid, private capital, and debt	ODA received as a % of GDP; net foreign direct investment flows as a % of GDP; total debt service as a % of GDP; HIPC decision point
1c The structure of trade	Balance of trade in goods and services
1d Economic performance over time	GDP per capita; GDP per capita annual growth rate as a %; fiscal deficit
Output	
2 *The Millennium Development Goals:* to assess the possible impact of the proposed import on progress in achieving the MDGs	Achieved; on track; lagging; far behind; slipping back

3 **Gender in development:** to gauge the possible impact of the diversion of social spending or the misuse of arms against women	The number of rural women living in conditions of economic underdevelopment and social marginalisation; the level of access to healthcare and related services; the prevalence of violence against women, including armed violence against women
4 **Security -** to assess the general security situation of the country	The number of IDPs; the number of refugees by country of asylum and country of origin; the rate of violent crime and existence of a pattern of unlawful killings/injuries

Factors: arriving at a judgement

1. Responsible governance

Security sector standards

Is there an informed, lawful, and transparent governance system in control of the security sector institutions?

Does the government observe civil and political rights as enshrined in the International Covenant on Civil and Political Rights?

Is there any credible evidence of the violation of the standards set in international humanitarian law within a ten-year period? Are the violations persistent, or even widespread and systematic? Does the government condone the violations? Are those responsible for the violations given impunity?

Responsible use of weapons

Does the government's past history demonstrate that it uses its weapons for lawfully stated needs; responsibly – according to international human rights and humanitarian law; without allowing them to be diverted; without widespread social and economic destruction?

Are the security personnel suitably qualified and trained to operate and manage the imported equipment lawfully?

Is there evidence of destruction of economic and social infrastructure by the use of weapons that was not proportionate to military objectives?

2 Arms procurement decision-making processes

Transparency and accountability

How transparent are state military expenditures and procurement? That is, to what degree is arms-procurement decision making in the importing country an open process?

Is there parliamentary oversight of the military procurement process, and are the parliamentarians adequately informed (is there a committee or hearing process, or are defence reviews conducted and are these open to public debate, for example)?

Are the armed forces and law enforcement agencies of the potential recipient sufficiently trained and accountable in terms of international humanitarian law (e.g. the Geneva Conventions) and international human rights standards (e.g. the UN Basic Principles on the Use of Force by Law Enforcement Officials)?

Corruption

Is there evidence of or suspicion of past corruption in government procurement practices?

Clarity

Is there a clear and consistent approach to military and law enforcement budgeting? In particular, does there exist a well-defined defence and law enforcement policy and a clear articulation of a country's legitimate security needs that is consistent with international law?

Development commitment

Has the state made development commitments such as poverty reduction targets consistent with its international obligations?

How successful has the government been in meeting these targets, or even attempting to address the country's most critical development needs?

Participation

Does there exist a national defence and law enforcement community to discuss, analyse, and make proposals regarding defence priorities in general, and arms acquisitions in particular?

Is arms-procurement information available to civil society groups, and are these groups able to participate meaningfully in arms-procurement decision making?

Does the arms budgeting process allow for input from government departments responsible for development targets (for example, the Ministry of Agriculture)?

3   *Rationale: appropriateness and affordability*

How appropriate is the import?

Does the imported equipment directly address security requirements consistent with development targets?

If not, how is the import justified in terms of security, political, or other needs, and are these justifications legitimate?

- If the import is justified in terms of security/political needs, is the strategy being pursued on the whole in a manner that is compatible with minimum global standards – for example in terms of compliance with UN resolutions, respect for international human rights standards, etc.?
- Even if this is so, is this the 'right' security strategy from a military/political point of view, given the government's overall strategic objectives? Or at least, is there a respectable case for it?
- Is the trade-off between security and other objectives the 'right' one?

In any case, is the import appropriate to the needs identified?

How affordable is the import?

Has the importing state conducted an extensive and comprehensive cost/benefit analysis of specific arms deals?

Has the importing state conducted an 'affordability study' or equivalent that assesses the impact of arms imports on other government programmes both in terms of immediate costs and also medium-and long-term costs?

Does the import represent an additional burden to the agreed military or law enforcement spending sector of the budget? If so, at the expense of which other sectors?

Is the cost of the import fair in terms of the equipment that it comprises and the stated needs of the importing state?

Will the import affect the medium- and long-term development goals of the PRSP, and/or of the MDGs for the country concerned?

What is the cumulative impact?

How does this impact change when the cumulative context is taken into account?

4   Importer capacity

Industrial and technological capacity

What is the level of industrialisation of the country in question?

How would the proposed import build upon the country's technological capabilities? For example, is there sufficient human capital to make any transfer of technology self-sustaining? Does the country have access to the necessary material resources to maintain and advance technology further? Would achieving such access be costly?

What would be the immediate and long-term impacts on the country's job markets and industrial growth?

Military/law enforcement technical capacity

Does professional law enforcement capacity exist at all levels to ensure the transfer is not diverted to illegitimate end users?

Does the appropriate infrastructure exist to make use of the imported equipment, for example, in terms of runways and roads or otherwise?

Are there personnel with the right skills and the management system to maintain the imported equipment?

Notes

1   See 'Guns and Policing', Amnesty International, Oxfam International, and the International Action Network on Small Arms, February 2004.

2   See www.worldbank.org/poverty/voices

3   This article also states that the 'Security Council shall be responsible for formulating, with the assistance of the Military Staff Committee referred to in Article 47, plans to be submitted to the members of the United Nations for the establishment of a system for the regulation of armaments'.

4   'Bleeding the Poor: Arms Versus Development', International Broadcasting Trust, 1994.

5   M. Gilbert (2000) *Challenge to Civilization: a History of the 20th Century 1952–1999*, HarperCollins; *The World Guide 2003/2004*, Oxford: New Internationalist Publications, 2003.

6   'Bleeding the Poor: Arms Versus Development', *op. cit.*

7   UNDP*, Human Development Report 2003.* It should be noted that the years given for comparison are not the same: figues are based on public expenditure on education from 1998–2000, or estimates from 1990 where this figure is missing; public expenditure on health in 2000, or in 1990 where this figure is missing; and military expenditure in 2001; all as a percentage of GDP. Only countries with low or medium development, as specified by the HDI, are listed.

8   R. F. Grimmett, specialist in National Defense, Foreign Affairs, Defense and Trade Division: *CRS Report to Congress,* 'Conventional Arms transfers to Developing Nations 1995–2002', September 22, 2003.

9   This definition is based on that used in the UN World Commission on Environment and Development, Brundtland Report (1987) *Our Common Future.*

10 For the Universal Declaration of Human Rights, see www.un.org/Overview/rights.html

    For the International Covenant on Economic, Social and Cultural Rights, see www.unhchr.ch/html/menu3/b/a_cescr.htm

11 Adopted by General Assembly Resolution 41/128 of 4 December 1986. This view was confirmed at the UN global conferences on population and development (Cairo, 1994) and women (Beijing, 1995) and at the World Summit on Social Development (Copenhagen, 1995).

12 See 'Millennium Development Goals in Reach by 2015: Proposed "Compact" Charts Way Forward', UNDP 2003, www.undp.org/hdr2003

13 'Missing the Target: the Price of Empty Promises', Oxfam International Policy Paper, July 2000.

14 UNDP, 'Millennium Development Goals: A Status Report', available at www.undp.org, complied in May 2003, data taken from the 2003 Human Development Report, for the occasion of the launch of the Report.

15 The majority of these statistics are taken from: *BICC Conversion Survey 2003 – Global Disarmament, Demilitarisation and Demobilisation*, Bonn International Centre for Conversion, Nomos Berlagsgesellschaft, Baden Baden. Information about the Millennium Development Goals is taken from: Millennium Development Goals, Regions, www.developmentgoals.org/About_the_goals.htm

16 Kofi Annan stated: 'What is needed… is not more technical or feasibility studies. Rather, States need to demonstrate the political *will* to carry out commitments already given and to implement strategies already worked out.' UNGA (2001) 'Roadmap Towards the Implementation of the UN Millennium Declaration', Report of the Secretary General, 6th September 2001, A/56/326.

17 'World 'failing poverty pledges'', BBC news website, Friday, 23 April, 2004, http://news.bbc.co.uk/2/hi/business/3651809.stm

18 It should be noted that prevalence is given in some places in this report to the case studies of India, South Africa, Ghana, Ethiopia, Tanzania, Croatia, Chile, Yemen and Venezuela because these cases represent those where it was either possible to undertake original research or collate secondary sources.

19 Human Development Report, UNDP 1994, p50. The HDRs include an index on resource-use that compares the percentage of GDP spent by a country on health and education to its military spending.

20 Sources: Ray Marcelo (2004) 'India poised to seal aircraft carrier deal', New Delhi, Financial Times, published January 19 2004 4:00; Admiral J. G. Nadkarni (retd.), 'Does India need to invest Rs9000 on a Russian aircraft carrier?', www.rediff.com/news/2000/jul/13nad.htm. The antiretroviral costs are based on US$150 per year per patient and taken from www.accessmed-msf.org/campaign/faq.shtm. See also: www.accessmed-msf.org/prod/publications.asp?scntid=22420041625454 &contenttype=PARA&

21 Y.P. Rajesh, 'Government approves purchase of Russian aircraft carrier', Reuters, 18 Jan 2004 13:41, www.reuters.com/locales/newsArticle.jsp?type=topNews&locale=en_IN&storyID=4153442

22 'World Bank's Statement on Tanzania's Air Traffic Control (ATC)', June 13 2002, available from http://web.worldbank.org

23 Mwesiga Baregu (2004) 'Military Procurement and Sustainable Development: The Case of the 'Watchman' Aircraft Control System in Tanzania', research undertaken for this report, p3.

24 Source: Emanuel Kwesi Aning (2004) 'Military Imports and Sustainable Development: Case Study Analysis – Ghana', research undertaken for this report, p18. (Interviews conducted by Aning at Danish Embassy, Accra, 15 December 2003; Japanese Embassy, Accra, 17 December 2003; and with DFID official, Accra, 18 December 2003.)

25 'Chile Does the Right Thing: Government Postpones f-16 Tender', *Arms Trade Insider* #45, Arms Trade Oversight Project, May 15 2001.

26 C. Wrigley, (2003) *The South African Deal: A Case Study in the Arms Trade*, Campaign Against the Arms Trade. It should also be noted that in contrast, McMillan (1992) and Rouy (1994) find that military spending in South Africa, while having a negative effect on economic growth, has not actually diverted resources from social spending. See P. Batchelor (1996) 'The economics of South Africa's arms trade' in J.Harker (ed.) *Collaborative Security in South Africa*, Aurora Papers 28, Ottawa: Canadian Council for International Peace and Security.

27 T. Crawford-Browne (2002) 'ECAAR: South Africa Challenges Arms Expenditures', in *ECAAR News Network*, 14:1, May 2002, p10.

28 B. Maclennan (2004) 'Arms deal challenge rejected', and 'ECAAR: SA to appeal arms ruling', 4 March 2004, Cape Town: iafrica.com, http://iafrica.com/news/sa/307387.htm

29 Fourth UN World Conference on Women, Beijing, 1995, 'Platform for Action'.

30 Ozren Žunec (2004) 'Croatia's Decision to Abandon the Upgrade of
    Mig-21 Aircraft with an Israeli Company', research undertaken for this report, p22.

31 Stephen Cviic (2003) 'Brazil opts for butter before guns', BBC website,
    www.bbc.co.uk, 4 January 2003, 01:50 GMT.

32 Declaration on the Right to Development, adopted by the General Assembly,
    Resolution 41/128 of 4 December 1986, Article 3 (3).

33 The full text of the Arms Trade Treaty can be viewed at:
    www.armslaw.org/documentos/armslaw/FrameworkConvention.english.pdf

34 See, 'Project on Sustainable Development and the Arms Trade Treaty, Literature
    Review', prepared by Kristiana Powell for Project Ploughshares, January 2004.

35 Cynthia Cockburn (1999) 'Gender, Armed Conflict and Political Violence',
    Washington DC: The World Bank, June 10 and 11 1999.

36 Of the 12 countries which have a high defence burden, with more than five per cent
    of their GDP dedicated to military expenditure, five, including the top two
    countries, are defined by UNDP as having low human development, according to
    'Human Development indicators 2002', UNDP website,
    http://stone.undp.org/hdr/repots/global 2002/en/indictor/indicator.cfm?File=
    index_indicators.html

37 Figures from 2000: net ODA US$1731m; military spend US$1686m.
    This figure for military spending is less than the actual amount, because much
    military spending is not included in national figures. While it cannot be assumed
    that Indonesia uses foreign aid to pay for imports directly – Indonesia has a
    diversified economy and many income streams – the point remains that the
    country is spending equivalent amounts on arms that it receives in aid.

38 'Foreign Report', Jane's Information Group, published on website 13 August 2002,
    http://www.janes.com/

39 See O.F. Adeola (1996) 'Military expenditures, health and education:
    bedfellows or antagonists in development?', Armed Forces and Society 22: 3,
    (Spring 1996) pp441–67; S. Willet (1999) 'The Arms Trade, Debt and
    Development', paper for Campaign Against the Arms Trade, May 1999; M. Knight,
    N. Loayza, and D. Villaneuya (1996) 'The Peace Dividend: Military Spending Cuts
    and Economic Growth', IMF Staff Papers, 43:1; Oyinlola Olaniyi (1998)
    'African economic integration and Nigeria's industrialisation: challenges for the
    defence sector', Defence Studies, volume 8 pp33–42.

40 D. Bockett (1999) 'Export or Expire: The Political Economy of the Post-Cold War
    Conventional Arms Trade', Occasional Paper No. 4, International Pacific College,
    New Zealand, June 1999; S. Goose and F. Smyth (1994) 'Arming genocide in
    Rwanda', Foreign Affairs 73: 5, pp86–96.

41 'Security, Poverty Reduction and Sustainable Development: Challenges for the
    New Millennium', the World Bank and the Belgian Ministry of Foreign Affairs,
    Foreign Trade and International Cooperation, September 1999.

42 'South Africa: Arms-deal chickens might be coming home to roost', Africa News,
    July 31 2003; 'Judgement reserved in arms deal case', Cape Town: South Africa,
    the article appears in the online Mail and Guardian, 18 February 2004
    (www.mg.co.za).

43 In South Africa, a realistic current estimate for the cost of a course of generic
    combination therapy for HIV/AIDS is around US$600 per year. According to
    UN AIDS 2002, there are five million HIV-positive South Africans.

44 Paul Watson (2003) 'Arms race leaves medicine behind; India and Pakistan spend billions on weapons while aid groups struggle for funds to fight polio and tuberculosis', *Los Angeles Times*, November 12 2003.

45 A report from the International Civil Aviation Organization, commissioned by the World Bank, states that a more appropriate system could have been bought for one tenth of the price, as discussed in Mwesiga Baregu (2004), 'Military Procurement and Sustainable Development: the Case of the "Watchman" Aircraft Control System in Tanzania', research undertaken for this report, p3.

46 As quoted in *Shattered Lives: the Case for Tough International Arms Control,* Oxfam International and Amnesty International 2003, p34. See also HM Treasury International Finance Facility proposal, January 2003, available at www.hm-treasury.gov.uk/documents/international_issues/global_new_deal/int _gnd_iff2003.cfm

The top ten developing-country arms purchasers for the years 1995–2002, according to the CRS Report to Congress, 'Conventional Arms Transfers to Developing Nations, 1995–2002', September 22 2003, were Saudi Arabia, Taiwan, Egypt, China, South Korea, UAE, Kuwait, Israel, India, and Pakistan. It should be noted that as used in the CRS report, the developing-nations category includes all countries *except* the United States, Russia, European nations, Canada, Japan, Australia, and New Zealand. According to the same report, in the earlier period (1995–1998), the value of all arms deliveries to Africa was over $2.7bn. In the later period (1999–2002), the value of all arms deliveries to Africa had decreased to about $800m (in current dollar values).

47 See, for example, Rachel Naylor (2000) *Ghana: An Oxfam Country Profile*, Oxford: Oxfam GB, p41.

48 Source: 'Secretary-General's Note for the Multi-Stake Holder Dialogue Segment of the Second Preparatory Committee, Addendum No. 1: Dialogue Paper by Women, Commission on Sustainable Development, Economic and Social Council', 28 January 2002, E/CN.17/2002/PC.Add.1.

49 Source: Emanuel Kwesi Aning (2004) 'Military Imports and Sustainable Development: Case Study Analysis – Ghana', research undertaken for this report, and discussion with the author 5 March 2004.

50 Sources: 'International Affairs: FY 2004 Budget', US Department of State Fact Sheet, Office of the Spokesman, Washington DC, February 3 2003, www.state.gov/r/pa/prs/ps/2003/17153.htm; 'Military assistance proposed 2004' (http://fas.org/asmp/profiles/aid/aidindex.htm#FY05cbj); Emad Mekay (2003) 'Foreign Aid Budget spotlights "war on terror"', *Inter Press Service,* February 3 2003; Jim Lobe (2004) 'Budget priorities reminiscent of Cold War', *Inter Press Service,* February 4 2004.

51 The UK Government, for example, undertakes 'life-cycle costs' assessments of all equipment that it purchases, as a matter of practice.

52 'Economic Cost of the Conflict in Northern Uganda', Civil Society Organisations for Peace in Northern Uganda, November 2002.

53 It is important to note that this conclusion is based on the assumption that economic growth is supported by economic and social-development expenditures. See D. P. Hewitt (1991) 'Military expenditures in the developing world', *Finance and Development,* 28: 3.

54 N. Ball (1988) *Security and Economy in the Third World,* Princeton: Princeton University Press; L. J. Dumas (2002) 'The role of demilitarization in promoting democracy and prosperity in Africa' in J. Brauer and J. P. Dunne (eds.) *Arming the South: The Economics of Military Expenditure, Arms Production and Arms Trade in Developing Countries*, New York: Palgrave.

55 Knight, Loayza, and Villanueva (1996) *op. cit.*; P. Collier and A. Hoeffler (2002) 'Military Expenditure: Threats, Aid and Arms Races', World Bank Policy Research Working Paper 29, 27 November 2002; D. P. Hewitt (1991) *op. cit.*; E. Lahera and M. Ortúzar (1998) 'Military Expenditure and Development in Latin America', *CEPAL Review,* No. 65, August 1998, p15–30; S. Willet (1999) *op. cit.*

56 A. Case (1994) 'Military Expenditure and Economic Development', Discussion Paper IPR86, Institute for Policy Reform, Princeton University, March 1994; D. Landau (1994) 'The impact of mlitary expenditures on economic growth in less developed countries', *Defence and Peace Economics*, 5: 3 pp205–20.

57 It should also be noted that in some cases, increased military expenditure gives a Keynesian boost to the economy, by increasing the GDP. However, such investment is wasteful because such "growth" is short-lived and does not lead to *sustained* economic growth. For a fuller description of this argument see: Amartya Sen, *Development As Freedom*, Oxford Paperbacks, 2001.

58 *Shattered Lives: the Case for Tough International Arms Control,* Oxfam International/Amnesty International 2003, p34.

59 'A Catalogue of Failures', Amnesty International, May 2003; O.F. Adeola (1996), *op. cit.*; S. L. Blanton (1999) 'Examining the impact of arms transfers on human development', *Journal of Third World Studies*, 16: 2, pp75–93; P. George (1998) 'Defense expenditures in the 1990s: budget and fiscal policy issues for developing countries: an overview', in 'Report 12: Converting Defense Resources to Human Development', Bonn International Center for Conversion, October 1998; P. Collier and A. Hoeffler (2002), *op.cit.*

60 P.O. Agbese (1992) 'With fingers on the trigger: the military as custodian of democracy in Nigeria', *Journal of Third World Studies,* Vol. 9, pp220–53; S. Deger (1986) *Military Expenditure in Third World Countries: The Economic Effects*, London: Routledge and Kegan Paul. See also J. Sislin and F. Pearson (2001) *Arms and Ethnic Conflict*, Lanham, MD: Rowman and Littlefield; and M. Wolpin (1986), 'Militarization, Repression and Social Welfare in the Third World', St. Martin's, New York.

61 As quoted in *Shattered Lives: the Case for Tough International Arms Control, op.cit.*, p31. See also, Amnesty International *et al.*, 'Guns and Policing', op. cit.

62 L. J. Dumas (2002), *op.cit.,* p17.

63 Source: 'Small Arms and Global Health', WHO contribution to the UN Conference on Illicit Trade in Small Arms and Light Weapons, July 9–20 2001, WHO/NMH/VIP/01.1. For more information, see also: www.who.int/violence_injury_prevention/violence/arms_landmines/arms/en/

64 'The Scorched Earth: Oil and Water in Sudan', Christian Aid, March 2001.

65 *Shattered Lives: the Case for Tough International Arms Control, op. cit.*, p45.

66 'European timber trader linked with Liberian arms trafficking', 16 July 2001, www.greenpeace.org/~forests

67 V. A. Farr (forthcoming) 'Death is everywhere: small arms and feminist anti-violence activism', *Women's Review of Books*.

68 As stated in *Shattered Lives, op. cit.*, p27. Original reference: F. Pickup with S. Williams and C. Sweetman (2001) *Ending Violence Against Women: A Challenge for Development and Humanitarian Work,* Oxford: Oxfam GB.

69 As stated in *Shattered Lives, op. cit.*, p27. Examples are cited in Wendy Cukier, 'Gender and Small Arms', Small Arms Firearms Education and Research Network (SAFER-Net), www.ryerson.ca/SAFER-Net/

70 As stated in *Shattered Lives, op. cit.* p27. Original reference: F. Pickup with S. Williams and C. Sweetman (2001), *op. cit.*

71 'Secretary-General's Note for the Multi-Stake Holder Dialogue Segment of the Second Preparatory Committee, Addendum No. 1: Dialogue Paper by Women, Commission on Sustainable Development, Economic and Social Council', 28 January 2002, E/CN.17/2002/PC.Add.1.

72 P. Dunne and S. Perlo-Freeman (2003) 'The demand for military spending in developing countries', *International Review of Applied Economics*, 17:1, pp23–48.

73 Jim Lobe (2002) 'Arms – Chile/US: concern over big F-16 sale', 'World News', *Inter Press Service*, January 10 2002.

74 'Arms race provides a fabulous market opportunity', and 'Blowing the barn door open: advanced weapons sales to Latin America', Federation of American Scientists, *Arms Sales Monitor* 35 August 1997, and 48 August 2002 respectively.

75 P. Watson (2003) 'Arms race leaves medicine behind; India and Pakistan spend billions on weapons while aid groups struggle for funds to fight polio and tuberculosis', *Los Angeles Times*, November 12 2003.

76 R. L. Sivard (1996) *World Military and Social Expenditures 1996*, Washington DC: World Priorities; T. Scheetz (1998) 'Transparency, accountability and rational decision-making in defense expenditures: the case of Argentina', in *Report 12: Converting Defense Resources to Human Development,* Bonn International Center for Conversion; R. Williams (1998) 'Reallocating defense expenditures for development: the South African experience', in *Report 12: Converting Defense Resources to Human Development,* Bonn International Center for Conversion, October 1998.

77 As stated in M. Bourne, M. Chalmers, T. Heath, N. Hooper, M. Turner (2004) 'The Impact of Arms Tranfers on Poverty and development', Centre for International Cooperation and Security, Department of Peace Studies, University of Bradford, p40.

78 See Amnesty International, *et al.,* 'Guns and Policing', *op. cit.*

79 J.P. Dunne (1996) 'Economic effects of military expenditure in developing countries: a survey,' in N.P. Gleditsch, O. Bjerkholt, A. Cappelen, R.P. Smith, and J.P. Dunne (eds.) *The Peace Dividend,* Amsterdam: Elsevier, p452.

80 DFID (2000) 'Summary: Aims and Outcomes', from *Security Sector Reform and the Management of Military Expenditure: High Risks for Donors, High Returns for Development,* report on an international symposium sponsored by UK Department for International Development, June 2000. Report available at: www.DFID.gov.uk/Pubs/files/ssrmes_report.pdf

81 Collier and Hoeffler (2002), *op. cit.*, pp12–13.

82 Emanuel Kwesi Aning (2004) *op. cit.*, p7.

83 See E. Hutchful (2002) *Ghana's Adjustment Experience: The Paradox of Reform,* Geneva: UNRISD, pp71ff.

84 While these negotiations were in progress, the Canadian government and the Royal Navy (UK) also offered to sell used vessels to the GN through their agents.

85 See 'Consideration of the Annual Estimates – Ministry of Defence', in *Parliamentary Debates* (Official Report) Fourth Series, 28: 41, col. 2946. The other services, including the Ghana Air Force (GAF), Military Hospital, and the Ghana Armed Forces' needs and activities were also given this developmental twist, see col. 2946ff.

86   *Ibid.*

87   See, for example, P. Batchelor and P. Dunne (2000) 'Industrial Participation, Investment and Growth: the Case of South Africa's Defence Related Industry', Cape Town: Centre for Conflict Resolution; Yong-Sook Lee and A. Markusen (2001) 'The South Korean defense industry in the ost Cold War era', in S. DiGiovanna and A. Markusen, (eds.) *From Defense to Development? Military Industrial Conversion in the Developing World,* forthcoming; G. Hammond (1990) *Countertrade, Offsets and Barter in International Political Economy,* New York: St. Martin's Press; L. J. Dumas, (ed.) (1995) *The Socio-economics of Conversion from War to Peace,* Armonk, New York: M.E. Sharpe; P. MacCorqudale, M. Gilliland, J. Kash, and J. and A. Jameton, (eds.) (1993) *Engineers and Economic Conversion,* New York, NY: Springer-Verlag; L.J. Dumas (1982) 'The conversion of military economy', in L.J. Dumas (ed.) *The Political Economy of Arms Reduction: Reversing Economic Decay,* Boulder, CO: American Association for the Advancement of Science and Westview Press; T. Crawford-Browne (1998) 'The R30 Billion Defence Procurement Proposals and Industrial Participation Programme (Offsets)', Cape Town: Coalition for Defence Alternatives; J. de Miramon (1985) 'Countertrade: an illusory solution', *The OECD Observer* Vol. 124, pp24–9; J. Sperling, D. Louscher, and M. Solomone (1995) 'A reconceptualization of the arms transfer problem', *Defense Analysis,* 11: 3, pp293–311.

88   Terry Crawford-Browne (former international banker, and chair of the South African affiliate of Economists Allied For Arms Reduction), 'Taking on the scams of the arms bazaar', Global News Wire Copyright 2003, *Africa Analysis,* September 5 2003.

89   C. Wrigley (2003) *The South African Deal: A Case Study in the Arms Trade,* Campaign Against the Arms Trade.

90   See: Controversial Radar a Success Story in Tanzania, *Fly South Aviation News,* www@flysouth.co.za

91   See, for example, Amnesty International, 'Catalogue of Failures', *op. cit.*, and Oxfam GB, 'Lock, Stock, and Barrel', February 2004.

92   G. Cawthra (2000) 'South Africa', in Ravinder Pal Singh (ed.) *Arms Procurement Decision Making Vol. II: Chile, Greece, Malaysia, Poland, South Africa and Taiwan,* New York, NY: Oxford University Press; S. Martin (1996) 'Countertrade and offsets: an overview of the theory and evidence', in S. Martin (ed.) *The Economics of Offsets: Defence Procurement and Counter Trade,* Amsterdam: Overseas Publishers Association; W. Struys (2002) 'Offsets in Small Countries: Between Scylla and Charybdis?', draft from ECAAR Conference on 'Offsets and Economic Development', Cape Town, 25–27 September 2002.

93   A. Markusen (2002) 'The Arms Trade as Illiberal Trade', paper for presentation and discussion at the Conference on 'Offsets and Economic Development', Cape Town, 25–27 September 2002, November 2002.

94   J. Brauer 'Economic aspects of arms trade offsets', in J. Brauer and P. Dunne, *Arms Trade and Economic Development: Theory, Policy, and Cases in Arms Trade Offsets,* London: Routledge (forthcoming 2004); K. Krause (1992) 'Arms imports, arms production, and the quest for security in the Third World', in B. L. Job (ed.) *The Insecurity Dilemma: National Security of Third World States,* Boulder, CO: Lynne Rienner Publishers; M. Brozska (1989) 'The impact of arms production in the Third World', *Armed Forces and Society,* 15: 4, pp507–30; R. Matthews (2002) 'Saudi Arabia: defense offsets and development', in J. Brauer and J. P. Dunne (2002) *op.cit.*

95 A. Markusen (2002) *op. cit.*

96 *Ibid.* See also A. Markusen (2001) 'Statement regarding offsets and US export controls', in Presidential Commission on Offsets in International Trade 2001, *Status Report of the Presidential Commission on Offsets in International Trade,* Washington, DC: Office of Management and Budget, January 18: Appendix H.

97 J. Brauer (forthcoming 2004) *op. cit.*

98 J. Brauer (1999); J. Brauer (forthcoming 2004);and Matthews (2002), *op.cit.*

99 N. Ball (1998) *Security and Economy in the Third World,* Princeton: Princeton University Press; Batchelor (1996) *op. cit.*

100 N. Ball (1988) *op. cit.*; L. Dumas (2002) *op. cit.*

101 Cawthra (2000) *op. cit.*

102 Batchelor (1996) *op. cit.*; Brauer (forthcoming 2004), *op. cit.*; Brzoska (1989) *op. cit.*

103 See Benoit (1973) and (1978); Frederiksen and Looney (1982) for earlier arguments; and J.P. Dunne (1996), and Scheetz (2002) for more recent work discussing the positive effects of military spending.

104 S. Deger and R. Smith (1983) 'Military expenditure and growth in less developed countries', *Journal of Conflict Resolution*, Vol. 27, pp335–53; E. Lahera and M. Ortúzar (1998) *op. cit.* See also N. A. Graham (1994) 'Introduction', in N. A. Graham (ed.)*Seeking Security and Development: The Impact of Military Spending and Arms Transfers,* Boulder, CO: Lynne Reinner Publishers, 1994.

105 Batchelor (1996) *op. cit.*, p114.

106 *Jane's Defence Weekly*, 30 May 2001.

107 Source: Binalakshmi Nepram (2004) 'From Non-violence to an Armed Nation: An Analysis of India's Military Imports Since the Cold War and its Impact on Sustainable Development', research undertaken for this report, p8.

108 See: H. Hughes, 'A Review of Current Practice on the Role of Sustainable Development in Arms Export Licensing Policy', Saferworld 2004.

109 Including the USA, the Russian Federation and such Eastern European states as Bulgaria, Romania, the Czech Republic, Poland and the Slovak Republic.

110 'Development Assistance Committee Guidelines: Helping To Prevent Deadly Conflict', OECD, 2001, pp38–9.

111 It should be noted that in the context of the EU Code of Conduct, the obligation on EU countries under operative provision three is to circulate 'details of licences refused … together with an explanation of why the licence has been refused'.

112 Trade and Industry Secretary Patricia Hewitt announcing the results of the interdepartmental review to the House of Commons on 1 August 2002.

113 *Ibid.*

114 The International Development Association, IDA, is the World Bank's concessional lending window. It provides long-term loans at zero interest to the poorest of the developing countries. The Government indicates that this list will be kept under constant review to take into account any changes to the list made by the World Bank of those states qualifying for concessional loans. States qualify for IDA if their per capita income is less than $875 for 2002 and in light of credit 'worthiness', that is the lack of financial ability to borrow from the International bank for Reconstruction and Development (IBRD). There is annual review of countries eligible for loans.

[115] Data is drawn from the World Bank's World Development Report. However, analysts are entitled to draw on other data as and when they see fit.

[116] The Dutch list covers more countries than that of the UK, including Middle Income countries since it draws upon DAC data. (The Development Assistance Committee (DAC) is the principal body through which the OECD deals with issues related to co-operation with developing countries). The UK only considers some of the Middle Income countries since it looks at the World Bank IDA list. http://www.dti.gov.uk/export.control/policy/criterion8.htm

[117] In spring 2003,the Senate attempted to raise notification thresholds to US$ 50 million for major defence equipment and US$ 100 million for general defence items. An earlier version of the same bill would have resulted in a much larger jump ($14 million to $100 million for major defence equipment, and from $50 million to $200 million for other defense articles.) However, the bill never passed. It is likely that the Senate will try to raise notification thresholds again in spring 2004.

[118] Stockholm International Peace Research Institute, 'Military Expenditure as a Share of GDP', http://projects.sipri.org/milex/mex_share_gdp.html (footnote a).

[119] Source: 'Elements for Objective Analysis and Advice Concerning Potentially Destabilising Accumulations of Conventional Weapons', approved by the 1998 Wassenaar Arrangement Plenary, 3 December 1998. www.wassenaar.org/docs/criteria.html

[120] In Sweden, before making a final decision, the licensing authority will hear evidence from the parliamentary export-control council.

[121] See Ken Epps, 'Project on Sustainable Development and the Arms Trade Treaty, Case Study Summary', Project Ploughshares, February 2004. This presentation of the case study analysis was adapted by Jane Chanaa.

[122] G. Cawthra (2000) *op. cit.*

[123] G. Pattillo (2002) 'The allocation of resources to the armed forces in Chile: a case of limited transparency', in J. Brauer and J. P. Dunne (eds.) (2002) *op. cit.*; F. R. Aravena (2000) 'Chile', in Ravinder Pal Singh (ed.) (2000) *op. cit.*; S. Perlo-Freeman (2003) 'Survey of Military Expenditure in South America', background paper for the *SIPRI Yearbook 2003*, available at http://projects.sipri.se/milex/mex_s_america_bg_03.pdf

[124] The Ghanaian Navy (GN) is a coastguard service and not a fighting service. Its main roles are fisheries protection, anti-smuggling and drug interdiction. Every acquisition by the GN is therefore in furtherance of these three roles which help in national development.

[125] Many countries are not currently in a position to complete fully the key steps to develop a PRSP. In order to prevent delays for countries seeking debt relief under the HIPC Initiative, an Interim PRSP (I-PRSP) can be formulated. An I-PRSP is meant to outline a country's existing poverty-reduction strategy and to provide a road-map for the development of the full PRSP (a timeline for poverty diagnostics, recognition of policy areas that need evaluation and reform, envisaged participatory process, etc.).

[126] Emanuel Kwesi Aning (2004) *op. cit.,* p10.

[127] Mwesiga Baregu (2004) *op. cit.,* p2.

[128] IRIN, 2 October 2003, 'Ethiopia: Pledge to Slash Defence Spending'.

[129] Derek B. Miller (2004) 'Country Study: Yemen', research undertaken for this report.

130 Ozren Žunec (2004) 'Croatia's Decision to Abandon the Upgrade of Mig-21 Aircraft with an Israeli Company', research undertaken for this report, p9.

131 Emanuel Kwesi Aning (2004) *op. cit.* pp13-14.

132 *Ibid.*

133 Derek B. Miller (2004) *op. cit.*

134 *Ibid.*

135 Cawthra (2000) *op. cit.*

136 Leenco Lata (2004) 'Arms Procurement and Ethiopia's Prospects for meeting PRSP and MDG Targets', research undertaken for this report, p5.

137 Binalakshmi Nepram (2004) *op. cit.,* p6.

138 Ken Epps, Project Ploughshares (2004), 'Case Study Summary,' p9.

139 Derek B. Miller (2004) *op. cit.*

140 M. Bourne, M. Chalmers, T. Heath, N. Hooper, M. Turner (2004) *op. cit.,* p44.

141 M. Robinson (2002) *Corruption and Development*, London: Frank Cass; C. Heymans and B. Lipiez (1999) 'Corruption and Development, Some Perspectives', *Monograph* No 40.

142 C. Courtney (April 2002) 'Corruption in the Official Arms Trade', Transparency International (UK), Policy Research Paper 001.

143 *Ibid.*

144 See Courtney (2002), *op. cit.*.

145 The Indian news portal *Tehelka* claimed on its website on March 13 2001, the Indian ruling party (Bharatiya Janata Party) chief, Bangaru Laxman allegedly accepted money from middlemen for an arms deal. See also 'Heads roll in Indian bribery scandal', BBC News 14 March 2001, http://news.bbc.co.uk/1/hi/world/south_asia/1219434.stm

146 See Ozren Žunec (2004) *op. cit.,* p15.

147 Ozren Žunec (2004) *op. cit.,* p2.

148 Binalakshmi Nepram (2004) *op. cit.,* p5.

149 N. Erik (1997) 'Recognition exacts a high price in arms', *Jane's Intelligence Review Pointer*, November 1997.

150 Ozren Žunec (2004) *op. cit.,* p7.

151 Derek B. Miller (2004) *op. cit.*

152 Mwesiga Baregu (2004) *op. cit.,* pp4–6.

153 In a press report on the court challenge of ECAAR-SA against the South African government, the government affordability study is quoted as noting that 'expenditures of this order will inevitably involve both a move away from government's existing fiscal targets and a significant restructuring of the national budget towards defence expenditure'. According to the press report, the government document also stated 'the most fundamental point that emerges from the risk analysis is that as expenditure increases the risks of the procurements escalate significantly … Relative to a situation where no arms were purchased, under the "combined adverse scenario", by 2008, GDP would be 1.6 per cent (R16bn) less, the budget deficit would be 0.8 per cent higher, there would be 115,000 fewer jobs, government would be spending 2.5 per cent more of its revenues on debt service, and the total public sector debt stock would be five per cent higher'. ('Finance Minister targeted in arms deal litigation', *South African Press Association*, February 17 2004.)

154 'The South African Deal', *op. cit.*, p13.

155 Binalakshmi Nepram (2004) *op. cit.*, p8.

156 Royal Navy press release, January 26, 2004.

157 This value was calculated by estimating that one single arms transfer should not be more than 1% of annual military expenditure, and global average military expenditure is approximately 2.75% of GDP. Thus one transfer should not be more than 1% of 2.75% of GDP – i.e. 0.0275% or more.

158 It is worth noting that attention to a 'governance approach' to military budgeting, which emphasises the study of the process rather than the level of military expenditure, has been taken up by the Stockholm International Peace Research Institute. This approach, which arose from DFID-sponsored discussions in 2000, 'combines good governance practices and sound financial management principles with security considerations and "focuses attention on the institutional framework for both managing trade-offs between different sectors and for the effective management of the resources devoted to the defence sector."' (Wuyi Omitoogun (2003) 'The processes of budgeting for the military sector in Africa', *SIPRI Yearbook 2003*, Oxford: Oxford University Press, p268.)

159 Organisation for Economic Co-operation and Development (OECD) Development Assistance Committee (DAC) meeting in Ottawa.

160 Wuyi Omitoogun (2003) *op. cit.*; DFID, 'Summary: Aims and Outcomes' from 'Security Sector Reform and the Management of Military Expenditure: High Risks for Donors, High Returns for Development', report on an international symposium sponsored by UK Department for International Development, June 2000. Report available at: www.DFID.gov.uk/Pubs/files/ssrmes_report.pdf. See also Part 2 of this report.

161 World Bank, GRICS II: Governance Research Indicator Country Snapshot at <http://info.worldbank.org/beeps/kkz/gov2001map.asp>

162 The International Monetary Fund in April 1998 adopted a 'Code of Good Practices on Fiscal Transparency', which is recognised as a framework of international standards for the conduct of fiscal policy. The work of the IMF and NGOs such as Transparency International (TI) would be instructive in assessing military-budget transparency. TI (UK),in particular, has developed six recommendations for 'reforming [arms] importing processes' including parliamentary and donor accountability, releasing bid criteria, and banning offsets. (See Courtney, *op. cit.*) The Corruption Perceptions Index of the Transparency International Global Corruption Report also would be a possible transparency indicator (see www.globalcorruptionreport.org/download.shtml).

163 In his chapter for the *SIPRI Yearbook*, Omitoogun identifies ten main elements of a proper budgeting process for the military sector. These include clear fiscal goals and responsibilities, defined challenges for the armed forces and the equipment required, proper accounting for expenditures, and audited outputs (Omitoogun (2003) *op. cit.*, p.270).

164 Chalmers points out a key predicament: the further analysis moves along this spectrum of questions, the more the analyser becomes deeply interventionist in ways that it is hard to justify in dialogue with developing country governments – especially since the answers to the latter questions may be coloured by the security interests of donor countries. However, there may often be cases, for example, where external aid (or debt relief) funds a large part of a government budget – as in Uganda. Here, one can argue more legitimately that this gives donors some more right to be heard as regards how their money is spent. At the same time, it also gives the donors more responsibility seriously to take into account the policy dilemmas faced by recipient governments, and to share responsibility with recipient governments for the consequences of their actions.

165 Such a study could be made mandatory if the value of the transfer is over a certain threshold, and should be able to prove that the importer government has attempted to balance all the relevant issues.

166 For this it is necessary to calculate: a - the current annual arms procurement/GDP, b - the five year average arms procurement/GDP. The percentage change is therefore: (a-b)/b as a percentage.

167 'Rio Declaration', 1992, A/CONF.151/26 (Vol. I), Report of the United Nations Conference on Environment and Development (Rio de Janeiro, 3–14 June 1992) Annex I. It should be noted that the development of modern international environmental law began in the 1960s, with principles for 'renewable resources' codified in the 1972 Stockholm Declaration on the Human Environment, including the elimination of weapons of mass destruction.

168 Declaration of the 1993 UN World Conference on Human Rights.

169 United Nations Development Programme (UNDP), *Human Development Report 1994*, New York, NY: Oxford University Press, p23. www.undp.org/hdro/1994/94.htm

170 On 1 May 2003, Sadako Ogata, former United Nations High Commissioner for Refugees, and Amartya Sen, Nobel laureate in economic science, presented the report of the independent Commission to the UN Secretary General, Kofi Annan. The Commission's report, 'Human Security Now: Protecting and Empowering People', can be accessed at www.humansecurity-chs.org/index.html

171 UN Fourth Global Conference on Women, (Beijing), 1995, Platform for Action.

172 The New Partnership for Africa's Development (NEPAD), October 2001. Its members include: Republic of Congo, Gabon, Cameroon, Kenya, Ethiopia, Mauritius, Egypt, Libya, Algeria, Tunisia, Mozambique, Botswana, South Africa, Nigeria, Senegal, Mali, and Ghana.

173 Profile: Intergovernmental Authority on Development, www.igad.org Member states include: Djibouti Somalia, Eritrea, Sudan, Ethiopia, Uganda, and Kenya.

Front cover photo; Crispin Hughes/Oxfam
Back cover photo: Giovanni Diffidenti/Oxfam

© Amnesty International, the International Action Network on Small Arms, and Oxfam International, June 2004.

This paper was written by Jane Chanaa of Oxfam GB, with major input from Debbie Hillier of Oxfam GB, Kristiana Powell and Ken Epps of Project Ploughshares and Helen Hughes of Saferworld. The draft text for this report has been extensively commented upon by Amnesty International and the University of Bradford's Department of Peace Studies - however the final published text in this report is the sole responsibility of the authors. The text may be freely used for the purposes of campaigning, education, and research, provided that the source is acknowledged in full.

Oxfam wishes to thank DFID for part-funding the work of the above-mentioned authors; the views presented herein do not necessarily represent the views of DFID or the UK government.

This report is a contribution to the initiative to promote the proposed Arms Trade Treaty. This initiative includes lawyers and many other NGOs and is convened by the Arias Foundation.

Copies of this report are available to download from
www.controlarms.org

Amnesty International is an independent worldwide voluntary activist movement working for human rights, with more than 1.5 million members, supporters and subscribers in over 150 countries and territories. It has national sections in 54 countries in every region of the world.
Email: info@amnesty.org.uk

The International Action Network on Small Arms is the global movement against gun violence - more than 500 civil society organisations working in 100 countries to stop the proliferation and misuse of small arms and light weapons. IANSA seeks to reduce the impact of small arms through advocacy, promoting the development of regional and thematic networks, supporting capacity building and raising awareness.
Email: contact@iansa.org

Oxfam

Oxfam International is a confederation of twelve development agencies which work in 120 countries throughout the developing world: Oxfam America, Oxfam-in-Belgium, Oxfam Canada, Oxfam Community Aid Abroad (Australia), Oxfam Germany, Oxfam Great Britain, Oxfam Hong Kong, Intermón Oxfam (Spain), Oxfam Ireland, Novib (the Netherlands), Oxfam New Zealand, and Oxfam Quebec.
Email: advocacy@oxfaminternational.org

www.ingramcontent.com/pod-product-compliance
Lightning Source LLC
Jackson TN
JSHW070242141224
75386JS00049B/1785